麦格希 中英双语阅读文库

探险之旅
第2辑

【美】波利佐罗斯（Polydoros, L.）●主编
张琳琳　汪洁　马洪娟●译
麦格希中英双语阅读文库编委会●编

全国百佳图书出版单位
吉林出版集团股份有限公司

图书在版编目（CIP）数据

探险之旅. 第2辑 /(美) 波利佐罗斯(Polydoros, L.) 主编；张琳琳, 汪洁, 马洪娟译；麦格希中英双语阅读文库编委会编. -- 2版. -- 长春：吉林出版集团股份有限公司, 2018.3（2022.1重印）
（麦格希中英双语阅读文库）
ISBN 978-7-5581-4771-5

Ⅰ.①探… Ⅱ.①波… ②张… ③汪… ④马… ⑤麦… Ⅲ.①英语—汉语—对照读物②故事—作品集—世界 Ⅳ.①H319.4：I

中国版本图书馆CIP数据核字(2018)第045989号

探险之旅　第2辑

编：	麦格希中英双语阅读文库编委会
插　　画：	齐　航　李延霞
责任编辑：	沈丽娟
封面设计：	冯冯翼
开　　本：	660mm×960mm　1/16
字　　数：	209千字
印　　张：	9.25
版　　次：	2018年3月第2版
印　　次：	2022年1月第2次印刷

出　　版：	吉林出版集团股份有限公司
发　　行：	吉林出版集团外语教育有限公司
地　　址：	长春市福祉大路5788号龙腾国际大厦B座7层
电　　话：	总编办：0431-81629929
	发行部：0431-81629927　0431-81629921(Fax)
印　　刷：	北京一鑫印务有限责任公司

ISBN 978-7-5581-4771-5　　定价：35.00元
版权所有　　侵权必究　　举报电话：0431-81629929

前言 PREFACE

英国思想家培根说过：阅读使人深刻。阅读的真正目的是获取信息，开拓视野和陶冶情操。从语言学习的角度来说，学习语言若没有大量阅读就如隔靴搔痒，因为阅读中的语言是最丰富、最灵活、最具表现力、最符合生活情景的，同时读物中的情节、故事引人入胜，进而能充分调动读者的阅读兴趣，培养读者的文学修养，至此，语言的学习水到渠成。

"麦格希中英双语阅读文库"在世界范围内选材，涉及科普、社会文化、文学名著、传奇故事、成长励志等多个系列，充分满足英语学习者课外阅读之所需，在阅读中学习英语、提高能力。

◎难度适中

本套图书充分照顾读者的英语学习阶段和水平，从读者的阅读兴趣出发，以难易适中的英语语言为立足点，选材精心、编排合理。

◎精品荟萃

本套图书注重经典阅读与实用阅读并举。既包含国内外脍炙人口、耳熟能详的美文，又包含科普、人文、故事、励志类等多学科的精彩文章。

◎功能实用

本套图书充分体现了双语阅读的功能和优势，充分考虑到读者课外阅读的方便，超出核心词表的词汇均出现在使其意义明显的语境之中，并标注释义。

鉴于编者水平有限，凡不周之处，谬误之处，皆欢迎批评教正。

我们真心地希望本套图书承载的文化知识和英语阅读的策略对提高读者的英语著作欣赏水平和英语运用能力有所裨益。

丛书编委会

Contents

Colonial Life
殖民生活 / 1

Pirates and Privateers
海盗与私掠者 / 8

Discovery in the Americas
发现美洲 / 28

The Reef
暗礁 / 47

The Story of Lewis and Clark I
路易斯和克拉克的故事（一）/ 80

The Story of Lewis and Clark II
路易斯与克拉克的故事(二) / 100

Vikings
维京人 / 121

1

◆ COLONIAL LIFE

Colonial Life

Step back more than three hundred years to when life was much different. *Imagine* a time before the United States was a country. It is a period known as the *Colonial* Times.

It is a cold morning. You wake up before the sun rises. You have much work to do. Only some lucky children get to go to school. Most kids spend their days working beside their parents.

殖民生活

让我们追溯到三百多年前的时代,当时的生活与现在非常不同。想象一下美国还不是一个国家的时候。我们把这个时代叫作殖民时代。

这天早晨很冷。太阳还没有出来,你就已经醒了。你要做的工作很多。只有非常幸运的孩子才可能上学。大多数的孩子每天都要和父母一起工作。

---

imagine *v.* 想象　　　　　　　　　　colonial *adj.* 殖民的

ADVENTURE TRIP II

♦ COLONIAL LIFE

You begin the day by washing up in the *washbasin* and getting dressed. The water isn't hot unless your mother or father has already boiled some. Then you light a lantern and walk outside to gather wood from the woodpile. This is your first chore of the day.

After you put the wood in the fireplace, a fire is lit to warm the house. Your mother uses the fire to cook breakfast. You soon sit down to a big breakfast. You need it because you have a day of hard work ahead of you.

If you are a girl, you probably have to help your mother cook, gather eggs from the chickens, or wash the laundry—by hand! You might also have to *churn* the butter. That means that you sit over a large wooden bucket full of cream. You grab a long, funny-shaped

---

你在脸盆里洗漱，然后穿上衣服开始了新的一天。如果父母不给你烧水，水也不热。然后你点上灯笼，到屋外的柴堆取一些柴，这就是你一天家务活儿的开始。

把柴放进壁炉，点着后为房子取暖。你妈妈用火煮早饭。很快你就会坐下来吃一顿饱饱的早餐。你必须吃得饱饱的，因为还有一天的重活等着你呢。

如果你是一个女孩，你可能要帮助妈妈做饭，拣鸡蛋，还要洗衣服——用手洗！你可能还要搅黄油，意思就是你要坐在一个大木桶上，木桶里装了满满的奶油。你握着一根长长的、形状很搞笑的棍子，轻轻地在

---

washbasin *n.* 脸盆　　　　　　　　　　　　churn *v.* 搅动

ADVENTURE TRIP II

stick and gently move it up and down in the bucket. This churns the cream until it slowly turns to butter. The butter tastes good, but it takes many hours to make. Once you make it, you are not able to keep it for long. You see, there are no *refrigerators* in colonial days. You have to *chill* things in a stream—if you live near one.

If you are a boy, you might have to work on the farm. You plant seeds and till soil with a plow pulled by oxen. You might repair the barn, milk the cows, or chop down trees for wood. Some days, you might help to build a new neighbor's house or even work in the local mill. You have to work many hours both in the cold of winter and in the heat of summer. There is no air conditioning in the summer. In the winter, you have only a fireplace to keep warm.

桶里上下搅动。就这样搅动奶油，直到它慢慢地变成黄油。黄油的味道很好，但需要很长的时间才能做出来，做好以后，也不能保存很长时间。你一定知道，殖民时代是没有冰箱的。你只得在小溪中给东西降温——如果你住的地方附近有小溪的话。

如果你是一个男孩，你可能得到农田里干活儿，你要播种，用牛拉的犁耙翻地。你可能还要修仓房、挤牛奶，或是砍柴。有时你可能还要帮助新邻居盖房子，或者要在附近工厂里做工。无论是在寒冷的冬天还是酷热的夏日，你每天都要工作很长时间。夏天没有空调，而冬天你只有壁炉取暖。

---

refrigerator n. 冰箱   chill v. 使变冷

◆ COLONIAL LIFE

You might come from a well-off family and attend school in a small, one-room *schoolhouse*. The classroom is filled with children of every age. One teacher has to teach all of the children. The subjects that you study are similar to what students learn in school today—math, reading, and writing. You do not study science.

You may be wondering if you have time for fun. The truth is that you spend most of your time working. In colonial days, there are no televisions to watch and no video games to play. You don't even have *electricity*.

If you don't go to school, you probably don't read. So reading a good book is not something you do for fun. Since people live far apart from each other, you don't have friends nearby. If you want to play with your friends, you don't have a bicycle to ride to their

---

你的家庭可能比较富有，你可能在只有一间小教室的学校上课，教室里各种年龄的学生都有。一名教师要教所有的学生，学的课程与今天学生们学得很像——数学、阅读和写作，那时不学科学。

你可能在想你有没有时间玩耍。事实上你大多数时间都用来工作。在殖民时代，没有电视看，也没有电子游戏可玩。甚至连电都没有。

如果你不上学，你可能也不需要读什么东西，所以读一本好书对你来说不是一件有趣的事情。由于人们相互住得都很远，所以附近也没有朋友。即使想和朋友一起玩耍，你也没有自行车骑到朋友家，你父母也没有汽车带你去。你不得不骑马或走一英里或更远的路。但是大多数的家庭成

---

schoolhouse *n.* 校舍   electricity *n.* 电

ADVENTURE TRIP II

houses. Your parents don't have a car to take you, either. You have to ride a horse or walk a mile or more. But most families are large. You probably have many brothers and sisters to play with.

On Sundays, children go to *church* with their families. This is a good day to play with your friends who also go to church. You might have picnics with other families in the afternoon.

Life in Colonial Times was much different from life today. It was a much harder life. People did not live long because there were no *medicines* or hospitals. But colonial life was also good in many ways. The air and water were much cleaner. There was not much traffic or noise.

Do you think you would like to have lived then?

员都很多，你可能有很多的兄弟姐妹一起玩。

星期日，孩子们都会和他们的家人一起去教堂。这是和你同去教堂的朋友们一起玩耍的好日子。你可以在下午同其他的家庭一起野餐。

殖民时期的生活与现在有很大的不同。那时的生活更加艰难。人们的寿命不是很长，因为那时没有药物，也没有医院。但是殖民时代的生活也有许多好的方面，空气和水比现在干净清澈，车流没有这么多，也没有噪音。

你觉得你愿意生活在那个时代吗？

---

church n. 教堂   medicine n. 药

◆ COLONIAL LIFE

ADVENTURE TRIP II

2

Pirates and Privateers

What do you think of when you think of *pirates*? Buried treasure? Ships with mighty sails? Black flags with a skull and crossbones?

Have you ever wondered what it was like to be a pirate? Pirates seemed to love adventure. They were often vicious men and women who were robbers and murderers. Pirates sometimes are *glamorized*

海盗与私掠者

想起海盗，你会想到什么呢？埋藏的珍宝？扬着巨帆的海盗船？有着骷髅和交叉骨头图案的黑色旗？

你可曾想过什么样的人能成为海盗呢？海盗们似乎喜欢冒险。他们常常是那些成为凶狠的强盗或谋杀犯的恶毒的男人或女人。电影和书籍有时候把海盗给美化了。实际上他们都是恶棍，他们的生活也并非那么快乐。

---

pirate *n.* 海盗　　　　　　　　　　　　　　glamorize *v.* 美化

♦ **PIRATES AND PRIVATEERS**

ADVENTURE TRIP II

in movies and books. But they were *scoundrels*, and the lives they lived were not that pleasant. Their lifestyles often resulted in great *discomfort* and even death.

The "Golden Age" of Pirates

Throughout history, pirates have sailed the seas all over the world. From the 1500s to the 1700s, many famous pirates raided ships and ports in the Caribbean Sea. This was called the "Golden Age" of pirates.

During the "Golden Age", Spain colonized large parts of Central and South America. The Spaniards were very interested in the spices, gold, and silver found in the Americas. In order to get these treasures, they forced the native people to work in mines and to gather spices. They also stole gold and silver from the native people.

他们的生活方式经常给他们带来痛苦，甚至是死亡。

海盗的"黄金时代"

纵观历史，海盗们已经在世界上所有的海洋中航行过。从16世纪到18世纪，有许多著名的海盗打劫了加勒比海的船只和港口。这就是所谓的海盗的"黄金时代"。

在"黄金时代"期间，西班牙把中美洲和南美洲的大部分地区变成了它的殖民地。西班牙人对在美洲发现的香料、黄金和白银非常感兴趣。为了得到这些珍宝，他们迫使当地人去矿山采矿或去收集香料。他们还从当地人那儿窃取黄金和白银。

---

scoundrel *n.* 恶棍　　　　　　　　　　discomfort *n.* 不适；痛苦

◆ PIRATES AND PRIVATEERS

The English and French *royalty* learned that Spain was getting rich from gold, silver, and spices from the Americas. They wanted gold for their empires, too. At the same time, there were a lot of *unemployed* sailors. The sailors were looking for adventure and a chance to get rich.

The Queen of England developed a plan to get some of the wealth the Spanish were bringing across the Atlantic Ocean on their ships. Her plan called for hiring unemployed sailors and providing them with ships to attack the Spanish ships. In England, these sailors were called privateers. In Spain, they were called pirates.

Many of the ships leaving the Americas loaded with riches

英国和法国王室知道了西班牙从美洲得到黄金、白银和香料，因此而变得越来越富有，他们想让自己的帝国也得到黄金。而此时，他们国家也有许多失业的水手。这些水手也在寻找冒险和致富的机会。

英格兰女王制订了一个计划——当西班牙的船队横渡大西洋时，从他们的船上夺取一些财宝。她这个计划需要雇用失业水手，并给他们提供船只去袭击西班牙船队。在英格兰，这些水手被称为私掠者。在西班牙，则被称为海盗。

许多离开美洲的船只都满载珍宝，穿过加勒比海。由于加勒比海域遍

---

royalty *n.* 王室   unemployed *adj.* 失业的

ADVENTURE TRIP II

passed through the Caribbean Sea. Since the Caribbean was full of small islands, it was a perfect place for pirates to hang out. It was also a perfect place from which to launch attacks on Spanish ships passing among the islands.

Pirates Attack!

Pirates quickly gained a reputation of being *ruthless villains*. Sailors on other ships were filled with fear when they saw a pirate ship approaching. They had heard tales of pirates and their nasty deeds. Most of the ships being attacked were cargo ships that lacked weapons for fighting off the pirates. The sailors knew there was little they could do to stop the pirates.

布小岛，因此是海盗出没的理想之地。要对经过小岛的西班牙船队发动袭击，加勒比海域也是个理想之地。

　　海盗袭击！

　　海盗们"残忍的恶棍"之名不胫而走。其他船只的水手们看到海盗船靠近就会感到十分恐惧。他们听说过海盗的故事和其恶劣的行为。大多数被袭击的船都是那些缺乏武器来抵御海盗的货船。水手们知道他们无法阻止海盗们的袭击。

---

ruthless *adj.* 残忍的 　　　　　　　　　　　　villain *n.* 恶棍

◆ PIRATES AND PRIVATEERS

Some pirates used smaller and swifter boats for night attacks. They would come alongside a cargo ship in the darkness of night. Then they would quickly seize the ship and kill many of the *unsuspecting* crew.

Before they boarded a ship, pirates fired a warning shot from a cannon. They hoped that the captain and crew of the ship would simply give up their cargo without a fight. Cannon shots were also used to destroy *masts* and *rigging* on the other ship. Pirates then threw smoke bombs onto the ship's deck to confuse and frighten the crew. The pirates then used grappling hooks to climb aboard the ship.

有些海盗用更小更快的船来发动夜间袭击。在黑夜里，他们能够靠近货船。接着，他们会迅速地夺船，并杀害那些毫无防备的船员。

海盗们登船前，会用大炮发送一声警告。他们希望船长和船员们能够不开战，就直接放弃货船。炮击也用来毁坏另一艘货船上的桅杆和绳索。然后，海盗们会把烟雾弹扔到货船的甲板上，来迷惑和恐吓船员。接着海盗们利用爪钩攀登到货舱上。

---

unsuspecting *adj.* 无戒备心的   mast *n.* 桅杆
rigging *n.* 绳索

Once on board, pirates used many kinds of weapons to take over a ship. One of the most common weapons was a cutlass. A cutlass is similar to a small sword. It was used for close-up, hand-to-hand fighting. Pirates also used guns, such as flintlock pistols and flintlock muskets. The muskets fired balls made of lead. The balls were loaded into the barrel one at a time and shot out with exploding *gunpowder*. Sometimes pirates made crude grenades that they used in their attacks.

Many people were wounded or killed in pirate battles. Sometimes, pirates would take *hostages*. They might even force members of a ship's crew to join the pirate crew. Usually, pirates would simply tie

---

海盗们一旦登上货船，就会用各式各样的武器来控制货船。最常用的一种武器是弯刀。弯刀和短剑很相像。它适合近身肉搏。有时海盗也用枪支，比如明火手枪和明火步枪。步枪发射出由铅制成的子弹。铅弹一次装进枪管一颗，发射出爆炸性的火力。有时海盗们也制造原油手榴弹用于袭击。

在与海盗的战斗中，有许多人会受伤或是被杀。有时，海盗还会劫持人质。他们还可能迫使船上的船员加入他们的团伙。一般情况下，海盗们

---

gunpowder *n.* 火药   hostage *n.* 人质

◆ PIRATES AND PRIVATEERS

up crew and passengers and then take anything of value to their ship. On occasion, pirates attacking in small boats would hijack the entire ship. These ships were then used to attack other ships.

It was the love of gold that caused most pirates—and the queens and kings who hired them—to steal. But pirates stole many other items of value. The ships that were attacked often carried silver and precious *gems*, such as *emeralds* and pearls. They also carried tobacco, wine, brandy, coffee, tea, spices, and expensive fabrics like *velvet* and *linen*. Pirates sold or traded most of these goods. They also kept some for their personal use.

只是把船员和船客绑起来，把所有值钱的东西抢到自己船上。只有在少数情况下，乘小船发动袭击的海盗们会抢劫整艘船。海盗们用抢劫来的船去袭击其他的船。

对黄金的热爱是大多数海盗以及女王们和国王们雇用海盗去偷盗的最初动机。但是海盗们也偷取许多其他有价值的物品。被袭击的船常常载着白银和绿宝石、珍珠等珍贵的宝石。船上也载着烟草、葡萄酒、白兰地、咖啡、茶以及像是丝绒和亚麻布这类昂贵的织物。海盗们把大部分的货物拿来出售或是以物换物。他们也留下一些给自己用。

gem *n.* 宝石
velvet *n.* 丝绒；天鹅绒
emerald *n.* 绿宝石
linen *n.* 亚麻布

ADVENTURE TRIP II

Life on a Pirate Ship

To some people, a pirate's life may seem exciting. But a pirate's life was not very *glamorous*. They were criminals who were hated as much as they were feared. They had to *constantly* be on guard and often couldn't even trust their fellow crew members. The work was hard and dangerous. Many pirates lost legs, arms, fingers, eyes, and even their lives in fierce battles. Living conditions were not very pleasant, either. They often lived in dirty, smelly quarters.

Pirates on a ship were assigned different jobs. One person was always assigned to stand watch. This person would cling to rope

---

海盗船上的生活

一些人觉得海盗的生活似乎很刺激。然而，海盗的生活并不是那么富有魅力。他们是其他人又恨又怕的罪犯。他们得不时地防范，甚至经常不能相信自己的同伴。这项工作很艰难，也很危险。许多海盗在激烈的战斗中失去了腿、手臂、手指、眼睛，甚至生命。他们的生活条件也并非那么舒适，住在肮脏、臭气熏人的尾舱是常有的事。

船上的海盗们有不同的分工。总有一个人被分配去站哨。这个人爬到远远高于甲板的绳梯去寻找他们要发动袭击的敌人或是船只。另外一个叫

---

glamorous *adj.* 富有魅力的 　　　　constantly *adv.* 始终；一直

◆ PIRATES AND PRIVATEERS

ladders high above the deck to look for enemies or ships to raid. Another person, called a *helmsman*, steered the ship with a lever called a tiller.

The *cooper* was the person who made, repaired, and sealed all of the barrels on the ship. Most of the food and drink was stored in barrels. The cooper had to make sure the barrels were well-made and sealed. Otherwise, the food or drink might go bad.

There were other jobs, too, like mending the sails, cooking for the crew, caulking the wooden deck planks, and pumping water from the bottom of the ship.

But when the work was done, pirates had time for eating, drinking, and entertainment. They ate meals together and drank

---

做舵手的人用叫作舵柄的控制杆来驾驶海盗船。

　　制桶工是制造、修补并密封船上所有桶的人。大多数食物和饮料都存贮在桶里。制桶工得确保那些桶做工良好、密封严实。否则，食物和饮料都有可能变质。

　　船上也有其他的工作，如修补船帆、为船员们做饭、堵上木质甲板上的裂缝以及从船底抽水这类的工作。

　　但是当这些工作完成时，海盗们就有时间吃饭、喝酒以及娱乐。他们一起吃饭，喝白酒或葡萄酒。他们玩掷骰子或是打纸牌这类游戏。他们也

---

helmsman　n.　舵手　　　　　　　　　　　　　cooper　n.　制桶工人

liquor or wine. They played games like dice or cards. They also played musical instruments, sang, and danced. Pirates were often lively and rowdy at mealtimes.

Like all sailors, pirates lived in close spaces with little privacy. They slept in *hammocks*. Their personal belongings, like shaving kits and clothing, were stored in sea chests.

Pirates often stole clothes from people on other ships. The crew dressed differently than the captain. They needed comfortable and practical clothes. A typical pirate wore simple shoes and pants, plus a waist *sash* and a jacket with wood or bone buttons. Crew members often wore *scarves* over their heads.

The captain usually wore much fancier clothing. Some captains

---

玩乐器、唱歌、跳舞。海盗们经常在吃饭时很活泼也爱吵闹。

和其他水手一样,海盗们生活在狭窄的空间里,几乎没有隐私可言。他们睡在吊床上。他们的个人物品,像是剃须工具包和衣物都存贮在水手储物箱里。

海盗们经常从其他船上的人那儿偷取衣物。海盗成员们跟船长的穿着有所不同。他们需要舒服实用的衣物。海盗的典型衣着是简单的鞋子、裤子,外加一根腰带和带有木质或骨制扣子的夹克。海盗成员头上还常常戴着头巾。

海盗船长通常穿着更昂贵的衣服。很多船长都喜欢穿丝质的裤子和有

---

hammock *n.* 吊床
scarf *n.* 头巾;围巾

sash *n.* 腰带

liked to wear silk pants and shirts with lace cuffs and gold buttons. They often wore shoes with silver buckles. Many pirate captains grew their hair long. They liked to tie it with ribbon to make it look like a gentleman's wig.

Not all pirates were men. There were a few women pirates, as well. Most pirate ships did not allow women on board, so women pirates had to *disguise* themselves by dressing like men.

Many pirate ship crews had a voice in the running of their ship. They voted on rules and helped decide how the treasure from raids would be divided. Of course, the captain always got the biggest share. Other shares were divided by the importance of a crew member's *responsibilities*. In some cases, crew members even

---

着花边袖口、金扣子的丝质衬衫。他们经常穿有银搭扣的鞋子。大部分海盗船长都留着长发。他们喜欢用丝带把头发绑起来，让它看起来跟绅士的头发一样。

并不是所有的海盗都是男的，也有一些女海盗。大多数的海盗船不允许女人们待在船上，因此女海盗们不得不女扮男装。

海盗船上的多数成员在经营海盗船上有发言权。他们按规定投票，帮助决定如何分配抢来的珍宝。当然，船长总是得到最大的份额。其余份额是根据成员责任的重要程度来分配的。在某些情况下，海盗成员甚至选举

---

disguise *v.* 伪装；假装   responsibility *n.* 责任

◆ PIRATES AND PRIVATEERS

elected the captain of their ship.

Well-known Pirates

Many pirates became well known. And many stories of these pirates have been passed down over the years. Let's look at some of the better-known pirates and the lives they led.

Blackbeard, whose real name was Edward Teach, was a *notorious* pirate born in England. He first served as a crew member on a pirate ship captained by a pirate named Benjamin Horngold. They attacked ships and port towns in the Caribbean. During that time, Blackbeard gained a *reputation* as a fierce fighter. *Eventually* Blackbeard went on to captain his own ship.

Blackbeard became one of the most feared pirate captains sailing

---

船上的船长。

著名的海盗

很多海盗很有名气。许多关于这些海盗的故事多年来一直流传着。让我们去看看这其中比较知名的一些海盗和他们曾经的生活。

真名叫爱德华·蒂奇的"黑胡子"是一个出生在英格兰的臭名昭著的海盗。他是在一艘由名叫本杰明·霍尼戈指挥的海盗船上开始了他的海盗生涯。他们在加勒比海袭击货船和港口城镇。那时,"黑胡子"赢得了凶猛斗士的名声。最后,"黑胡子"开始指挥他自己的船。

"黑胡子"就成了航行在加勒比海上最让人恐惧的海盗船长之一。

---

notorious *adj.* 臭名昭著的   reputation *n.* 名声
eventually *adv.* 最后;终于

ADVENTURE TRIP II

the Caribbean. Rather than wait for his victims to take off their rings and give them to him, Blackbeard would cut off their fingers. He would place burning, smoking flares in his beard. Black smoke would rise around his face, causing people to think he was mad or crazy. That made him even scarier.

In 1718, Blackbeard and his crew sailed up the Atlantic coast of America and into North Carolina. At that time, North Carolina was part of the British colony. Blackbeard sailed up coastal rivers and raided wealthy *plantations*.

People were scared and angry. They wanted to *get rid of* Blackbeard and his pirates. They asked the British Navy for help. A British Navy captain and his crew fought a fierce battle with

---

"黑胡子"不会等着受害人自己拿下他们手上的戒指交给他,就会砍下他们的手指。他把燃烧着冒着烟的火焰放到胡子上。黑烟会上升笼罩着他的脸,不由得让人们认为他是个疯子。这使他更让人觉得恐怖。

在1718年,"黑胡子"和他的海盗团伙航行到美国大西洋沿岸,进入北卡罗来纳。那时,北卡罗来纳是英国殖民地。"黑胡子"航行到沿海河流,将富裕的种植园洗劫一空。

人们很害怕,也很愤怒。他们想要摆脱"黑胡子"和他的海盗团伙。他们向英国海军求助。英国海军上校和他的船员们与"黑胡子"一伙展开

---

plantation *n.* 种植园   get rid of   摆脱

◆ PIRATES AND PRIVATEERS

Blackbeard and his crew. Blackbeard lost his life in that battle. According to legend, it took 20 cutlass wounds and five shots to kill him.

Anne Bonny was one of a few women pirates. She was born in Ireland. She moved to South Carolina with her family when she was a young girl. Her father was a lawyer, and her mother was a *maidservant*. Anne fell in love with a sailor and ran away with him to New Providence, in the Bahamas. Then she met the pirate Calico Jack and joined his pirate crew.

She disguised herself as a man and was a tough fighter. Most people did not know she was a woman. She raided ships with Calico Jack until 1720. They were eventually *captured* by the British Navy

---

了激烈的战斗。"黑胡子"战死在这场战斗中。据传说,用弯刀刺了20下,又开了5枪才杀死了"黑胡子"。

安妮·邦妮是为数不多的女海盗之一。她出生在爱尔兰。她小时候就和家人搬到南卡罗来纳。她的父亲是一位律师,母亲是一位女仆。安妮和一名水手相爱了,并和他一起私奔到了位于巴哈马群岛的新普罗维登斯岛。后来她遇到了海盗"棉布杰克",加入了他的海盗团伙。

她把自己伪装成一个男人,一个坚强的战士。多数人不知道她是一个女人。在1720年以前,她还和"棉布杰克"一起劫船。他们最后被英国

---

maidservant n. 女仆 　　　　　　　　capture v. 俘虏;捕获

ADVENTURE TRIP II

and were tried in a court in Jamaica. The judge first sentenced Anne to death by hanging. But before the hanging, the Navy learned that she was *pregnant*. Her sentence was then changed to life in prison.

Pegleg is another well-known pirate. He worked as a privateer for a French king. He is best known for his "wooden leg". But Pegleg, whose real name was François le Clerk, did not have a wooden leg. Instead, he used a wooden *crutch* after losing his leg in a battle. Pirates with wooden legs are often popularized in movies and books, such as *Treasure Island*, probably because of Pegleg.

Captain Kidd was another famous English pirate. When he was

海军抓获，在牙买加接受法庭审判。开始法官判处安妮绞刑。但在实行绞刑前，海军得知她有了身孕。因此她由死刑改成了无期徒刑。

佩格勒是另一名知名的海盗。他是一名为法国国王服务的私掠者。他以他的"木腿"而出名。但是真名叫佛朗索瓦·勒克莱尔的佩格勒却没有木腿。相反，他在一次战斗中失去腿后，开始用木制拐杖。有木腿的海盗们在电影里、小说里通常会很流行，比如说《金银岛》，可能就是因为佩格勒而受欢迎。

基德船长是另一位知名的英格兰海盗。他最终被捕处死后，当局政府

---

pregnant *adj.* 怀孕的   crutch *n.* 拐杖

◆ PIRATES AND PRIVATEERS

finally captured and put to death, the *authorities* ordered his body to be hung by the harbor for all to see. This was done to discourage others from becoming pirates.

Another privateer was Sir Francis Drake, an Englishman. He started sailing when he was just 14. He first sailed with his cousin John Hawkins, who took *slaves* from Africa to the Americas.

Sir Francis began to captain his own ship in 1570. He attacked Spanish ships, stealing large amounts of treasure for Queen Elizabeth of England. Sir Francis did not limit his pirating activity to the sea. When he learned that the Spanish were taking more riches

---

命令把他的尸体吊在港口，让所有的人都来看。这样做是为了打消其他人想要当海盗的念头。

另一名私掠者弗朗西斯·德雷克爵士是一个英国人。他14岁就开始航海。他首次航行是和他的表兄约翰·霍金斯一起。他的表兄把非洲的奴隶运送到美洲。

弗朗西斯·德雷克爵士在1570年开始指挥他自己的船只。他袭击西班牙船队，为英格兰女王伊丽莎白窃取了大量的珍宝。弗朗西斯爵士的海盗行为并非仅限于海上。当他得知西班牙人通过运货的骡队从巴拿马的矿

---

authority *n.* 当权者；当局   slave *n.* 奴隶

ADVENTURE TRIP II

from mines in Panama by mule train, he went inland and attacked the *mule* trains. He even captured the town in the center of the mining region. Sir Francis Drake became a rich and successful pirate by attacking ships and mule trains. Queen Elizabeth rewarded Drake for capturing so much treasure for England by making him a *knight*.

Conclusion

During the Golden Age of piracy, no ship was safe on the sea. The Caribbean Sea was one of the most notorious hangouts for pirates. But pirates sailed the seas in other parts of the world as well.

Pirates were often lawless, vicious men and women who made

山获得更多财富时，他去内地抢劫了骡队。他甚至占领了位于矿区中央的城镇。弗朗西斯·德雷克爵士通过抢劫货船和骡队，成了一位富有的成功的海盗。伊丽莎白女王授予德雷克爵士称号，因为他给英格兰夺取了大量的珍宝。

结论

在海盗行为的黄金时代，没有一艘船在海上是安全的。加勒比海是最臭名昭著的海盗出没地之一。然而海盗们也航行到世界其他地方的海域。

海盗总是那些藐视法律、凶狠的人，他们通过偷窃、抢劫来维持生

---

mule *n.* 骡子　　　　　　　　　　　　　knight *n.* 爵士；骑士

◆ PIRATES AND PRIVATEERS

their living by stealing and robbing. Other pirates were ex-sailors hired by kings and queens who were greedy and wanted more wealth.

Modern-day pirates still *roam* the seas of the world. But rather than sailing slow wooden sailboats, they have high-powered speedboats. They attack small pleasure boats and ships. They steal *valuables* that they can then sell on the black market.

计。其他的海盗曾是水手，后受国王和女王们雇用，他们贪得无厌，总想要得到更多财富。

今日的海盗仍然徘徊在世界各大海上。他们不再驾驶着速度缓慢的木制帆船，他们有马力强大的快艇。他们袭击小游艇和货船。他们偷取贵重物品然后在黑市上出售。

---

roam *v.* 徘徊 valuable *n.* 贵重物品

ADVENTURE TRIP II

3

Discovery in the Americas

CHAPTER 1: Christopher Columbus

In 1492, Columbus sailed the ocean blue.

This is a famous *rhyme* about a famous voyage. On August 3, 1492, Christopher Columbus set sail from Europe with a group of three ships. He was looking for a *shortcut* to a group of islands in Southeast Asia called the Indies. That's why he tried to sail west across the Atlantic Ocean.

发现美洲

第一章：克里斯托弗·哥伦布

1492年，哥伦布航行过大海之湛蓝。

这是一首关于一次著名航行的押韵诗。1492年8月3日，克里斯托弗·哥伦布率领由三艘船组成的船队，从欧洲出发开始了这次航行。他在努力地寻找到达东南亚群岛的捷径，那里被叫作印度群岛。所以他要试图向西横渡大西洋。

---

rhyme *n.* 押韵短诗   shortcut *n.* 捷径

◆ DISCOVERY IN THE AMERICAS

Columbus didn't realize that large *continents* would block his way. He and his crew spotted land on October 12. They thought it was the Indies.

But instead, it was a place that Europeans had never seen before. These continents became known as the Americas.

Every year in October, the United States *celebrates* the feats of Christopher Columbus. Many people say that Columbus discovered the Americas. But other people disagree. They say that he wasn't the first to discover this land.

So did Columbus really "discover" the Americas? Discovery

哥伦布并没有意识到广阔的大陆会阻挡他们。他和船员在10月12日看到了陆地。他们认为那就是印度群岛。

然而，那是一个欧洲人从未见过的地方。这些大陆后来被称作美洲。

每年10月，美国都会庆祝克里斯托弗·哥伦布的这一丰功伟业。许多人认为是哥伦布发现了美洲。但是另一些人却不这么认为。他们认为，哥伦布并不是发现这片大陆的第一人。

真的是哥伦布"发现"了美洲吗？发现的含义是某物第一次被找到

---

continent n. 大陆　　　　　　　　　　celebrate v. 庆祝

is when something is found or seen for the first time. But was Columbus really the first person to walk on the American continents? Had anyone come before him?

The Vikings

Some people say that Columbus wasn't even the first European to arrive in America. The Vikings, sailors and *warriors* from northern Europe, may have explored the northern part of the Americas years before Columbus set sail. The Vikings discovered many northern lands, including Iceland and Greenland. A possible Viking landing site has been discovered in Canada. It is nearly 1,000 years old.

Columbus was not the first person to set foot in the Americas.

或看见。那么哥伦布真的是踏上美洲大陆的第一人吗？在他之前有人来过吗？

北欧海盗

一些人认为哥伦布甚至不是到达美洲的第一个欧洲人。北欧海盗，来自于欧洲北部的水手和勇士们，他们可能在哥伦布开始航海之前就已经探索了美洲的北部。北欧海盗们发现了许多北部的陆地，包括冰岛和格陵兰岛。北欧海盗可能登陆过的遗址在加拿大被发现，距今将近1000年。

哥伦布并不是踏上美洲的第一人。一些民族已经在那里生活了几千

---

warrior *n.* 勇士

ADVENTURE TRIP II

People had been living there for thousands of years. These people had already made pottery, built *pyramids*, and studied *astronomy*. Many different civilizations were already there.

Now you will learn about three groups of people—the Maya, the Anasazi, and the Inca. The Maya built cities in the *rainforest*. The Anasazi built houses in the sides of cliffs. And the Inca had cities high up in the mountains. You will read about how and where they lived in the Americas. You will also figure out when they lived. This will help us answer our question: Did Columbus actually discover the Americas?

年。这些人已经会制陶、建金字塔和研究天文。许多不同的文明已经在那里存在。

现在你将了解到三个种族的人——玛雅人、阿那萨齐族人和印加人。玛雅人在雨林里建城。阿那萨齐族人在悬崖边儿建造房子。而印加人在高山上建造了城市。你将了解到他们是如何、在美洲大陆上的何处生活的。你也将了解到他们生活在哪个时期。这将有助于我们找到问题的答案：真的是哥伦布发现了美洲吗？

---

pyramid *n.* 金字塔   astronomy *n.* 天文学
rainforest *n.* （热带）雨林

◆ DISCOVERY IN THE AMERICAS

CHAPTER 2: The Maya

Thousands of years ago, the Maya built giant stone pyramids in the Central and South American rainforest. Some pyramids were as tall as ten-story buildings, with steps going all the way up. Priests walked up the steep steps with offerings for the gods. At the top were temples for *religious* ceremonies.

The Maya knew a lot about architecture, astronomy, art, math, and writing. They studied the stars and made calendars. They carved big sculptures and painted bright *murals*. Their math system used dots and bars instead of numerals. Their writing used pictures

---

第二章：玛雅人

几千年前，玛雅人在美洲中部和南部的雨林里建造了巨石金字塔。一些金字塔高达10层楼，有台阶可以通往顶端。祭司带着献给众神的供品走上陡峭的台阶。在顶部，坐落着举行宗教仪式的庙宇。

玛雅人懂得很多建筑、天文、艺术、数学和文字书写方面的知识。他们研究星群，制定了日历。他们雕刻了巨大的雕像，绘制了鲜艳的壁画。他们在数学体系中使用圆点和横条，而不是数字。他们的文字表达使用图画和符号，而不是用单词和字母。玛雅人把文字写在石头上，也写进书

---

religious *adj.* 宗教的   mural *n.* 壁画

ADVENTURE TRIP II

and symbols instead of words and letters. The Maya wrote on stone surfaces and in books made out of *fig* tree paper. A few of these books still exist today.

The Maya were farmers who grew crops such as corn, beans, and chili peppers. They liked to eat flat corn cakes, which are now called tortillas (tor-TEE-ahs). The Maya raised turkeys and hunted animals like deer. They traded *jaguar* skins, jade, and brightly colored bird feathers. At religious festivals, the Maya danced and had feasts.

Most Maya cities had large ball courts. These courts had walls with stone rings high above the ground. They used these courts to

里，纸张是用无花果树制成的。其中一些书保存至今。

玛雅人以务农为主，他们种植玉米、豆子和红辣椒。他们喜欢吃那种薄的玉米饼，现在叫作墨西哥薄馅饼。玛雅人养火鸡，并且狩猎，如捕鹿。他们做豹皮、翡翠和彩色羽毛的贸易。在庆祝宗教节日时，玛雅人载歌载舞，尽情吃喝。

大多数的玛雅城市都有很大的球场。球场的墙壁上镶有石环，这些石环远远地高于地面。他们在这些球场里玩一种受尊重的运动，参与者要把

fig n. 无花果   jaguar n. 美洲豹

◆ DISCOVERY IN THE AMERICAS

ADVENTURE TRIP II

play a sacred game in which players hit a rubber ball through the ring. But they weren't allowed to use their hands. They had to hit the ball with their hips, shoulders, and *thighs*.

Remaining Ruin: Chichén Itzá

For hundreds of years Chichén Itzá was the most powerful Maya city. It had a huge open plaza and a giant pyramid. There were also many other buildings, including a steam bath and an *observatory* for studying the stars. Chichén Itzá was also home to the largest ball court in the area.

Chichén Itzá is not just a name from the past. You can still find

---

一只橡皮球碰进石环里。但是，他们不能用手碰球，只能用臀部、肩膀和大腿。

遗址：奇琴伊查城

几百年来，奇琴伊查一直是最强大的玛雅城市。那里有一个很大的开放广场和巨大的金字塔。还有许多其他建筑，包括蒸汽浴房和用来观察星群的天文台。那个区域最大的球场也在那里。

奇琴伊查不只是一个古时的名字。如今在南墨西哥，你仍能找到它。

---

thigh *n.* 大腿　　　　　　　　　　　　　　observatory *n.* 天文台

it in southern Mexico. Many of its pyramids still exist. Tourists walk up these old pyramids. They also study the detailed stone carvings. Some sit by the ball court and imagine what the games were like. Nearby, there are even more ruins. But these are still buried under soil, plants, and trees.

CHAPTER 3: The Anasazi

The story of the Anasazi is amazing and *mysterious*. The Anasazi were also known as the "cliff *dwellers*" or the "ancient ones". They lived in the Southwestern region of today's United States. These people lived as hunters and then as farmers, growing corn, beans,

---

它的许多金字塔保存至今。游客会走上这些古老的金字塔，也会研究精细的石雕品。一些人坐在球场边上，想象着那些游戏是怎么玩的。附近还有更多的遗址。但是，它们仍被埋在土壤、植物和树木下面。

第三章：阿那萨齐族人

阿那萨齐族人的故事充满了魅力和神秘。阿那萨齐族人也被称作"悬崖上的居住者"或者是"古老的居住者"。他们住在如今美国的西南地区。阿那萨齐族人最初以狩猎为生，之后开始务农，他们种植玉米、豆

---

mysterious *adj.* 神秘的   dweller *n.* 居民；居住者

ADVENTURE TRIP II

squash, and cotton. They built sandstone houses in the sides of cliffs. But about 700 years ago, the Anasazi simply vanished from their homes.

Today we know about the Anasazi because they left many clues behind. It seems as if they left one day, meaning to come back. But they never did. Their *sandstone* houses were still intact. Clothes hung from hooks, and pottery lay on the ground. *Archaeologists* later found sandals, baskets, blankets, and garden tools. There were many pieces of beautiful pottery, such as jars and bowls with black and

子、南瓜和棉花。他们在悬崖边上建筑砂岩房子。但是，大约700年前，阿那萨齐族人从他们的家园消失了。

如今，我们能了解阿那萨齐族人，是因为他们留下了很多线索。他们似乎在某一天离开了家园，打算再回来，可是他们再也没有回来。他们的砂岩房子仍保存完整。衣服挂在挂钩上，陶器放在地上。后来，考古学家发现了凉鞋、篮子、毯子和园艺工具。还有许多漂亮的陶器，如有红黑相

sandstone *n.* 砂岩　　　　　　　　archaeologist *n.* 考古学家

◆ DISCOVERY IN THE AMERICAS

red designs. The Anasazi also left *petroglyphs* of people and animals carved into rock walls.

Why did these people leave their homes so suddenly? To this day, it is still a mystery. Some people believe that a long drought made it too hard to grow food there. Others believe that the Anasazi were suddenly *invaded*.

We do know that some Anasazi traveled southeast and settled there. Today's Pueblo people in New Mexico are *descendants* of the ancient Anasazi.

间设计的罐子和碗。阿那萨齐族人将人物和动物雕刻在岩石上，留下了岩石雕刻。

阿那萨齐族人为什么突然离开了他们的家园？直到今天，这仍是个谜。一些人认为，长期的干旱使人们无法种植食物。其他人认为，阿那萨齐族人遭到了突然入侵。

我们确定的是，阿那萨齐族人向东南部走了，并定居在那里。如今新墨西哥的普艾布罗人就是古老阿那萨齐族人的后代。

---

petroglyph *n.* 岩石雕刻；岩画　　　　　　　　　　invade *v.* 入侵；侵略
descendant *n.* 后代

ADVENTURE TRIP II

Remaining Ruin: Mesa Verde

You can still find signs of the Anasazi today. Perhaps the most amazing Anasazi ruins are at Mesa Verde National Park in Colorado. Many tourists visit this site every year. They walk through ancient houses built into the sides of cliffs.

The most famous ruin is called Cliff Palace. It sits under a big rocky ledge. There are stairs, courtyards, and rooms packed together. Circular rooms called kivas remain where the Anasazi held *ceremonies*. In the museum you can see *authentic* Anasazi pottery and baskets.

遗址：梅萨维德

如今，你仍能找到阿那萨齐族人的痕迹。也许，最有魅力的阿那萨齐族人遗址就是位于科罗拉多州的梅萨维德国家公园。每年都有游客来此参观，他们徘徊于这些悬崖边上古老的房子中间。

最有名的遗址叫悬崖宫。它坐落在一块大的岩脊下面。那里有楼梯，庭院和一排排的房屋。叫作基瓦的圆形房屋仍被保存在阿那萨齐族人曾举行过仪式的地方。在博物馆，你能看到真正的阿那萨齐族人使用过的陶器和篮子。

---

ceremony *n.* 仪式　　　　　　　　　　　authentic *adj.* 真正的

CHAPTER 4: The Inca

The Inca lived along the western edge of South America. They built a large and rich empire. The Inca empire covered thousands of miles of jungles, mountains, and beaches.

The Inca were good builders and engineers. They built a network of stone roads that connected towns. They even built long *suspension bridges* over rivers and *canyons*. Before the age of telephones and cars, they kept in close contact. Messengers ran between towns to relay messages from far away.

The Inca were also master farmers. They cut terraces into steep

---

第四章：印加人

印加人居住在南美洲的西岸。他们构建了庞大且富裕的帝国。印加帝国覆盖了几千英里的丛林、山脉和海滩。

印加人是出色的建筑师和工程师。他们建立了连接城镇的石路交通网。他们还在河流和峡谷上搭起吊桥。在电话和汽车时代来临之前，印加人就能够保持紧密联系。信使来往于城镇间，传达着远方带来的消息。

印加人也是务农高手。他们在陡峭的山上割出了梯田。这样他们就可

---

suspension bridge 吊桥   canyon n. 峡谷

mountainsides. This gave them flat places to grow food. They also dug *irrigation* canals that brought water to their crops. They grew corn, cotton, potatoes, and quinoa. Llamas helped the Inca carry things up the mountains.

Today relatives of the Inca still live high in the green Andes. On steep, sloping lands they grow foods like quinoa. Some still speak the ancient language, Quechua, and live like their Inca ancestors. Music groups play drums and make beautiful, haunting sounds with traditional flutes. Today musicians from Ecuador and Peru play popular Andean music all around the world.

以在平坦的土地上种植食物。他们挖灌溉水渠，从而把水引到庄稼地里。他们种植玉米、棉花、土豆和藜麦。美洲驼可以帮助他们把食物运到山上。

  如今，印加人的后代仍住在郁郁葱葱的安第斯高山上。在陡峭的斜坡上，他们种植食物，如藜麦。一些人仍旧说古老的语言，盖丘亚语，并且像他们的印加祖先那样生活。乐队会敲鼓，用传统的笛子吹出优美的让人难以忘记的声音。如今，来自厄瓜多尔和秘鲁的音乐家们会演奏受全世界欢迎的安第斯山音乐。

---

irrigation *n.* 灌溉

◆ DISCOVERY IN THE AMERICAS

Remaining Ruin: Machu Picchu

Machu Picchu is one of the most *impressive* ruins in the Americas. It is an ancient Inca city built out of stone. It is *perched* high on a green mountaintop in Peru. Machu Picchu is so *isolated* that the outside world didn't know about it until 1911. Machu Picchu may have been a home for a royal family.

The "Inca Trail" is a famous stone path that still leads to Machu Picchu. Today tourists from all over the world travel to Peru to hike the Inca Trail. They follow a four-day route over high mountain passes. They also walk by other Inca ruins. At the end, hikers arrive at a stunning view of Machu Picchu.

遗址：马丘比丘

马丘比丘是美洲最壮观的遗址之一。它是用石头建筑的古代印加城。它坐落在秘鲁的绿色高山上。马丘比丘与世隔绝，直到1911年才被外界所了解。马丘比丘可能是当时一个皇室家族的住所。

"印加小路"是一条有名的石铺小路，至今仍通往马丘比丘。如今来自世界各地的游客到秘鲁观光，都会攀爬这条小路。游客在四天的行程里，攀越高山要隘；他们也会参观其他印加遗址。最后，徒步旅行者会到达马丘比丘，一睹那里令人叹为观止的风光。

---

impressive *adj.* 给人深刻印象的   perch *v.* 置于
isolated *adj.* 偏远的

ADVENTURE TRIP II

CHAPTER 5: Point of View

Now you have learned about different people from the Americas. You know about the Maya, the Anasazi, and the Inca. So let's go back to our *original* question. Did Columbus really discover the Americas?

Columbus arrived in 1492. More than fifty years before that, the Inca empire was already *flourishing*. In 1200, the Anasazi lived at Cliff Palace. And long before all of that, the Maya were building giant pyramids.

It is clear that many people lived in the Americas before 1492. Columbus himself even wrote about the local people he met. When Columbus first arrived, he thought he had landed in the Indies.

第五章：观点

现在，你已经了解到来自美洲的不同民族——玛雅人、阿那萨齐族人和印加人。那么让我们回到最初的那个问题，真的是哥伦布发现了美洲吗？

哥伦布是在1492年到达美洲的。而在这之前的50多年前，印加帝国已经处在繁荣时期。1200年，阿那萨齐族人居住在悬崖宫上。并且，在那很久以前，玛雅人已经开始建造大金字塔了。

显而易见，在哥伦布1492年到达美洲之前，许多人已经居住在那里。哥伦布甚至亲自记录了他所见到的当地人。当他初次在那里登陆时，

---

original *adj.* 最初的；原先的   flourish *v.* 繁荣

◆ DISCOVERY IN THE AMERICAS

That's why he *mistakenly* called the local people "Indians". For many years, the people from the Americas have been called Indians. But now more people call them Native Americans. This is because they are native to the Americas. Their families have lived here for many years.

If you want to learn more about Native Americans, you can study their ruins. You already know that Chichén Itzá is in Mexico, Cliff Palace is in Colorado, and Machu Picchu is in Peru. These ruins are proof of the people who lived in the Americas before Columbus. If you are lucky enough to visit the ruins, you may meet Native American people in those areas. It was their *ancestors* who built these cities long ago.

他认为那里是印度群岛。这就是为什么他误把那里的人称作"印第安人"。多少年以来，来自美洲的人们被称作"印第安人"。但是现在更多的人称他们为"美洲土著人"。这是因为他们是美洲的原始居民。他们和家人已经在那里居住了很久。

关于美洲土著人，如果你想了解更多，你可以研究他们的遗址。你已经知道墨西哥的奇琴伊查、科罗拉多州的悬崖宫，还有秘鲁的马丘比丘。这些遗址都能证明，在哥伦布之前，他们就生活在美洲。如果你能幸运地参观到这些遗址，你也有可能遇到仍居住在那些遗址附近的美洲土著人。是他们的祖先很久很久以前在那里建筑了城市。

---

mistakenly *adv.* 错误地   ancestor *n.* 祖先；祖宗

ADVENTURE TRIP II

So why do people still say that Columbus discovered the Americas?

Well, the answer to this question probably depends on *perspective*. Perspective is the point of view from which you see something. From the perspective of the Europeans, Columbus had found new land. So for them, it was a discovery.

But from the perspective of the Native Americans, Columbus hadn't discovered their land. These people had already been eating, sleeping, and farming there for many years. So depending on the perspective, both sides could be right. Maybe we could better say that Columbus explored the Americas. That's probably more *accurate* than saying he discovered them.

那么为什么人们仍认为是哥伦布发现了美洲呢？

如此看来，问题的答案很可能因角度不同而不同。角度是指看待事情的立足点。从欧洲人的角度来看，是哥伦布发现了新大陆。对他们来说，那是一个发现。

但是从美洲土著人的角度来看，哥伦布并没有发现他们的大陆。因为这些人已经在那里吃、住和耕种了许多年。所以依据不同的角度，两种看法可能都是正确的。也许，我们最好说，是哥伦布探索了美洲大陆。这样的说法，要比"是哥伦布发现了美洲"的说法更准确。

---

perspective *n.* 观点；思考方法　　　　accurate *adj.* 准确的

4

The Reef

The following is three months of a journal kept by Will Reynolds, a *fictional* crew member of The Endeavour, a ship *commissioned* by the King of England and captained by the famous English explorer Captain James Cook. Captain Cook made three voyages to the Pacific Ocean, mapping the islands and exploring New Zealand and Australia.

暗礁

以下是由威尔·雷诺兹记录的为期三个月的航海日志,他是"奋勇号"中一名虚构的船员。"奋勇号"是由英国国王委任并由著名英国探险家詹姆斯·库克船长率领的一艘轮船。库克船长曾三次出海前往太平洋地区,探索途中绘制了岛屿地图,并探索了新西兰和澳大利亚。

---

fictional *adj.* 虚构的　　　　　　　　　　commission *v.* 任命

ADVENTURE TRIP II

◆ THE REEF

Sunday, April 1, 1770: I am now beginning the second book of my journal. Should the first book be lost, these are the facts.

My name is Will Reynolds and I am a *crewman* on His Majesty's Ship, The Endeavour, captained by the honorable James Cook. We set sail from Plymouth, England, on August 25, 1768. I am an assistant to Mr. Joseph Banks, an *esteemed naturalist* whose job is to collect *samples* of plants and describe any animals we see.

We reached Tahiti on April 13, 1769. The Captain and the scientists made some observations of the planets. They were also supposed to make observations that would help determine the distance of the Earth from the sun.

1770年4月1日，星期日：我现在开始写第二本航海日志。第一本日记可能已经丢了，我有以下事实证明。

我叫威尔·雷诺兹，是英国皇家海军——"奋勇号"的一名船员。该船由声誉卓著的詹姆斯·库克船长率领。1768年8月25日，我们从英格兰的普利茅斯出航。我负责协助受人尊敬的博物学家约瑟夫·班克斯，他的工作是采集植物样本，并描述我们见到的所有动物。

1769年4月13日，我们抵达塔希提岛。库克船长和科学家们对行星进行观察。他们也希望能做一些观测，以帮助我们计算出地球与太阳的距离。

---

crewman *n.* 船员　　　　　　　　　esteem *v.* 尊重；敬重
naturalist *n.* 博物学家　　　　　　sample *n.* 样本

ADVENTURE TRIP II

The crew tried to make friends with the natives, which was very easy. The natives are *extremely* friendly. Some of the men wanted to stay with the women they had fallen in love with. We were treated well and made to feel welcome. They willingly shared food and taught us what was *edible* and what was poisonous.

We also surveyed the island and built a fort that future British sailors could use.

So far, we have lost only six men, and none to sicknesses such as *scurvy*. Two men have drowned. One died of too much rum. One jumped overboard. Two men died during bad weather in Tierra del Fuego, where we had stopped for supplies and water before

---

船员们很快与当地人交上了朋友。这些当地人非常友好。有些船员甚至想在这里留下来，陪着他们爱上的姑娘。我们受到了热情的款待，当地人愿意分食物给我们吃，还告诉我们什么是能吃的，什么是有毒的。这一切都让我们感到自己很受欢迎。

我们也考察了这个岛屿，还建了堡垒，方便以后到这里来的英国船员使用。

到目前为止，共有六名船员丧生，不过没有人死于疾病——比如坏血病。六人中有两个人溺水而死，一个人饮酒过量而死，一个人跳海自杀，还有两个人死于火地岛的恶劣天气。火地岛是我们穿越太平洋前驻足下来

---

extremely *adv.* 非常   edible *adj.* （无毒而）可以吃的
scurvy *n.* 坏血病

beginning the journey across the Pacific Ocean. These last two were friends of mine, as we were all assigned to serve Mr. Banks.

We have been circling New Zealand, creating coastal maps for nearly six months now. The men have enjoyed the chance to collect fruits from the land. When we are at sea for longer periods, we must eat the Captain's *regimen* of onions, salted cabbage, *marmalade* of carrots, *sauerkraut*, and other things of which we know nothing. The stuff tastes terrible, except for the lemons. He insists these things will stave off the scurvy. And if we don't eat some of them daily we get a lashing.

On the Captain's orders, we have raised anchor and are leaving this land. The men believe we are heading home, at last, though no

---

准备食物和水的地方。最后提到的两位是我的朋友，我们都是负责协助班克斯先生的。

六个月来，我们一直环绕新西兰航行，并绘制沿海地区的地图。船员们很享受在岛上采摘水果的时光。我们出海时间较长的时候，就要遵从船长的养生食谱——吃洋葱、腌白菜、果酱萝卜、泡菜，还有一些我们听都没听过的东西。除了柠檬，那些东西都很难吃。船长坚持认为吃那些东西可以暂时防止坏血病，而且要是我们某天没吃养生食谱上的东西，就会遭到鞭打。

船长一下命令，我们就拉上锚准备离岛。船员们都以为即将踏上返程

---

regimen *n.* 养生法　　　　　　marmalade *n.* 橘子酱；酸果酱
sauerkraut *n.* （酸）泡菜

ADVENTURE TRIP II

word has come from the Captain. I would like to return to my wife and little girl. It has been such a long time since I have seen them.

Thursday, April 5: The winds are calm today, but we are still making progress.

Few of the crew can read or write. I am often lonely. Mr. Banks talks to me about his work, and lends me his books to read from time to time. There isn't a lot of time to rest, but when there is, most of us sleep for lack of any *amusement*.

I have been writing letters to my daughter, Chelsey, throughout the *voyage*. When last I saw her she was three years old. I want her to know about the years I was away from her, and that I was thinking of her.

之旅，虽然船长始终没有说过。我想回到妻子和小女儿身边。我已经很久没见过她们了。

4月5日，星期四：今天，海风很平静，不过我们还得继续前进。

船员中没有几个人会读书写字，所以我经常觉得孤单。班克斯先生给我讲工作上的事，还经常借我书看。我们没多少休息时间；有时间休息时，大家也只是睡觉，因为根本没有什么娱乐活动。

在整个航行过程中，我一直给女儿切尔西写信。她三岁以后我就没见过她了。我想让她知道，在我离开她的那么多年里我都做了些什么，并让她知道我很想念她。

---

amusement *n.* 娱乐活动　　　　　　　　　　　voyage *n.* 航行

◆ THE REEF

Thursday, April 12: We tried to catch fish using bits of salted meat for bait. We didn't catch anything.

The sea was smooth and calm today. Mr. Banks went to shore in his boat to collect samples. He shot several birds, including a red-tailed *tropical* bird that we have seen each of the last few days. From the sea, he netted a bluish jelly-like mass called a Portuguese man-of-war. These creatures are known for their powerful stings, so he handled it carefully, lest he be stung. An *albatross* that Mr. Banks shot seems to eat these bluish stinging creatures. I am at a loss to understand why anything would eat these *hideous* blobs. Their stings are worse than those of a wasp.

4月12日，星期四：我们尝试用腌肉做诱饵抓鱼，但一条都没抓到。

今天，海面风平浪静。班克斯先生乘船到岸上采集样本。他射到了几只鸟，包括一只红尾热带鸟，最近我们每天都能看见这种鸟。他还在海里网住了一只僧帽水母（为淡蓝色透明囊状物）。这种生物以其强大的蜇伤力而闻名，所以班克斯先生小心翼翼地拿着它，唯恐自己被蜇到。他射下来的一只信天翁倒好像想吃那只僧帽水母。我想不通为什么会有东西喜欢吃这些可怕的水团。僧帽水母的蜇伤力可比黄蜂厉害多了。

---

tropical *adj.* 热带的　　　　　　　　　albatross *n.* 信天翁
hideous *adj.* 十分丑陋的；别人厌恶的

ADVENTURE TRIP II

We work mostly in four-hour shifts. The Captain has provided the men with woolen trousers and jackets to keep us warm. He believes there is no reason to lose a man to any kind of sickness on a voyage. He takes care of us, and the men are very loyal because of his kindness.

We do sometimes object to his need for everything to be cleaned so often, but it gives us something to do for the hours we aren't on deck.

Friday, April 13: Every man was on his best behavior today. They are *superstitious* of this day being bad luck. No one was willing to climb to the crow's nest today. There were no *accidents*.

我们通常是4小时换一次班。船长给我们拿了羊毛裤和夹克来御寒。他觉得不应该有任何一名船员在航行中因疾病而丧生。他把我们照顾得很好，也因为他的和蔼仁慈，大家对他很忠诚。

有时候，我们确实很讨厌翻来覆去地清洗每一样东西，不过好处就是我们不在甲板上时，总算有些事情可做。

4月13日，星期五：今天每个人都挺守规矩的。大家都很迷信，相信这一天会有厄运。没人愿意自找麻烦。也没有意外发生。

---

superstitious adj. 迷信的   accident n. 意外

◆ THE REEF

We spotted a large group of flying fish today, confirming that we are in tropical waters. A larger fish that we could not see was chasing the flying fish. Mr. Banks tried to net the creature that was chasing the fish but without success.

Monday, April 16: Some thunder just after sunset tonight. First sign of bad weather in days. Many birds visited the ship this evening, including a small land bird the size of a *sparrow*. The men tried to catch it, for amusement I would guess, but lost it in the rigging and never saw it again.

Wednesday, April 18: We sighted a group of *porpoises* today, at

---

今天我们看到一大群飞鱼，由此我们确定已经到了热带水域。有一条大鱼在追赶飞鱼，但我们看不清那条大鱼。班克斯先生试着网住大鱼，不过没能抓到。

4月16日，星期一：太阳刚刚落山就听到了打雷声。这是多日以来天气要变糟的第一个征兆。晚上有许多鸟飞到船上，包括一只像麻雀一样大的陆地鸟。船员们可能是要找个乐子，想抓住那只雀鸟，但鸟落在绳索上时他们没抓住，后来就再没看见过。

4月18日，星期三：今天我们看到了一群鼠海豚，至少有八只。它们

---

sparrow *n.* 麻雀   porpoise *n.* 鼠海豚

ADVENTURE TRIP II

least eight. They threw their whole bodies several feet above the water's surface as they swam alongside our ship.

Thursday, April 19: We sighted land today just after dawn. In the afternoon the crew were called up on deck to witness three *waterspouts* moving between the land and us. We are nearly five or six leagues (about 17 miles/28 km) from shore. One of the spouts lasted a good quarter of an hour, with a thickness near that of the ship's mast. It seemed to *descend* from a mass of gray cloud and was surrounded by mist and rain. The ocean beneath it was very *agitated*.

Captain Cook believes we are on the Eastern Shore of New Holland. He intends to map this coast, since it is the only unmapped

---

在我们轮船旁边游动时，整个身体能够飞离海面几英尺。

4月19日，星期四：一清早，我们就看到了陆地。下午，全体船员都被召集到甲板上，看着在陆地与我们之间形成的三道海龙卷。我们离海岸将近五六里格（约17英里或28千米）。其中一道厚厚的海龙卷持续了整整15分钟，在船的桅杆附近一直盘旋。海龙卷被迷雾和大雨包围着，仿佛要从一大团灰云中掉下来似的。下方的海水也被它搅动得波涛汹涌。

库克船长相信，我们已经到了新荷兰的东海岸。他想要将这个海岸线

---

waterspout *n.* 海龙卷   descend *v.* 下来
agitated *adj.* 激动的

◆ THE REEF

coast of this land. The Captain decided to sail north along the coast, without dropping *anchor* to gather fruits and allow the men some time off the ship. We are all disappointed, but there is work to do and we will do it.

Friday, April 20: Several clouds of smoke were spotted rising from the forests beyond the *coastline*. In the evening several more were spotted. Maybe it is good that we have not gone ashore.

Sunday, April 22: This morning we spotted five men on the beach. On the hill beyond the beach we could make out several small houses. The men all appeared to be very black. They looked at

---

绘制进地图，因为这是此地唯一一条未被绘制的海岸线。船长没有抛锚让船员们去摘水果，也没有留出时间让船员下船休息，他决定沿着海岸线向北航行。我们都有点失望，不过既然有事要做，还是做正事要紧。

4月20日，星期五：有烟雾从离海岸线很远的森林里升起。晚上，烟雾越来越多。或许我们决定不上岸是很明智的。

4月22日，星期日：今天早上，我们发现海滩上有五个人。从海滩望过去的山上，我们清晰地看到几座小房子。这些人看起来都很黑。他们看

---

anchor *n.* 锚　　　　　　　　　　　　coastline *n.* 海岸线

ADVENTURE TRIP II

us as though they had never seen white men before. Perhaps they have.

Thursday, April 26: The land today appears more *barren* than any we have seen before. The shore consisted mostly of chalky cliffs, not unlike those of old England. The site made more than a few of the crew members feel *homesick*.

Friday, April 27: Mr. Banks, the Captain, and Dr. Solander tried to go ashore in the ship's small boat called a yawl. The Pinnacle, our longboat, was judged too leaky to float. We did not get to land, fearing the surf too rough for our small boat.

Saturday, April 28: We spotted several small canoes carrying two men each. They landed and met with their friends on shore. All of

---

着我们，那眼神好像之前他们从来没有见过白人。也许他们见过。

4月26日，星期四：今天我们见到的土地似乎比以前见过的都更贫瘠。海岸主要由白垩质的悬崖构成，跟旧时英国的悬崖很相似。这情景使许多船员开始想家。

4月27日，星期五：班克斯先生、船长和索兰德医生设法乘"奋勇号"带的小艇上岸。我们的大划艇"山巅之船"漏水太严重，不能在海上继续航行了。我们其余人没有到岸上去，怕小艇经不起汹涌的海浪。

4月28日，星期六：我们发现了几只独木舟，每只独木舟上都有两个人。他们登陆，和岸上的朋友见面。这些人似乎都是男性，每个人都带着

---

barren *adj.* 贫瘠的   homesick *adj.* 思乡的；想家的

◆ THE REEF

ADVENTURE TRIP II

these appeared to be men, and well armed with swords and spears. They were all naked, but their bodies were painted with broad white *stripes* on their faces, chests, and legs.

The Pinnacle, patched up overnight, was sent ahead to scout. Upon returning, the officer said that the natives had invited them *ashore* with many words and hand gestures that were not understood.

Later in the afternoon, we sailed by a small village consisting of six or eight houses. An old woman, followed by some children, was seen coming out of the woods and entering one of the houses. Some other women were spotted working at the surf's edge, and having seen our ship, paid no attention to us as we passed. A little

---

剑和长矛，全副武装。他们全部赤身裸体，但他们的脸上、胸部和腿上都画有很宽的白色条纹。

我们的"山巅之船"经过彻夜的修整，被送往前方去侦察。船上的长官一回来，就说当地人邀请他们上岸，但是当地的语言很不好懂，手势语也无法沟通。

下午晚些时候，我们驶过一个小村庄，村子里有六或八户人家。几个孩子跟在一个老太太身后，从树林里出来，进入其中一户人家。还有些女人在岸边干活儿，她们看到了我们的船，但当我们的船从她们眼前驶过时，她们却根本没在意。过了一会儿，有几只独木舟到岸，那些人便开始

---

stripe *n.* 条纹   ashore *adv.* 上岸

◆ THE REEF

later some of the canoes came ashore and a fire was lighted with which to cook their dinner. It was observed, especially by some of the crew, that all the people, men and women, were naked.

In the evening, we loaded up our boats and went ashore, hoping to be little noticed by the natives. Two men, warriors by appearance, came to meet us with harsh language we could not understand and waving lances at us. Although we *outnumbered* them greatly, they made great protest at our desire to come ashore.

We tried to assure them we only wanted some water and fruit, but they were unmoved. So we fired a *musket* over their heads. At this the younger man dropped his lances and ran, but then returned and began to yell some more. The Captain then ordered a load of

---

点火做饭。有一些船员特别注意到，他们所有人，无论男女，都是裸着的。

晚上，我们装载完货物便上了岸，希望不要被当地人注意。有两个外表很像武士的男人，向我们走过来，说了些我们听不懂的话，还朝着我们挥着长矛。尽管在人数上我们占有很大的优势，但他们还是强烈抗议我们上岸。

我们向他们保证只要些水和水果，但他们根本不理。我们只好用火枪向他们头上开了一枪。这时，年轻一点的人扔下长矛就跑了，不过一会儿又返回来，开始更用力地大叫起来。然后船长命令小范围朝他们开火。有

---

outnumber *v.* 数量上超过   musket *n.* 火枪

ADVENTURE TRIP II

small shot to be fired at them. It hit the older man in the legs, but did not seem to bother him much. He ran to a house and returned with a *shield*.

Two more loads were fired and this was enough to scare the men away. We went ashore and walked up to one of the houses. There were several small children *huddled* behind a shield. We tossed some beads, ribbons, and clothing through the window and continued on our way. We collected as many lances as we could find, nearly 40 or 50, and they were all tipped with very sharp fish bones.

The people here are darker than any we have seen. They seem lean and quick and healthy. We can only imagine what they might think of our straight hair, pale skin, and heavy clothing.

一个年长的老人腿上中了一枪，但他也没什么反应。他跑进屋里，回来时手里多了个盾牌。

我们又射了两膛子弹，这下可把他们吓跑了。我们上了岸，走进其中一家。几个小孩儿挤在一个盾牌后面。我们从窗户向里扔了一些玻璃珠、丝带和衣服，然后继续前进，我们把能找到的长矛都收走了，大概有四五十把，而且每一根都是用非常锋利的鱼骨头做的箭头。

这里的人是我们所见过的肤色最黑的。他们看起来瘦弱、敏捷、健康。至于他们会怎样看待我们的直发、白皮肤和厚重的衣服，我们就只能自己想象了。

---

shield *n.* 盾　　　　　　　　　　　huddle *v.* 挤在一起

◆ THE REEF

Sunday, April 29: We went ashore again today for water. The sky is very blue, and it is still warm here. It feels like the season is starting to turn, though, so I hope we will be heading home soon.

The natives *approached* as we collected water, but retreated as soon as we sent two men to meet them.

They watched us from a safe distance. After a while they collected their canoes, moved them above high tide, and carried two others away with them. We approached the houses and found all of our gifts just as they had fallen.

Monday, April 30: More *encounters* with the natives, but no real contact. They try to scare our men with yelling and display of weapons. There seems to be nothing we can do to assure them we

---

4月29日，星期日：我们今天又上岸去取水喝。天空蔚蓝，此地还是很热。但是有种快要换季的感觉，所以我希望我们很快就会启程回家了。

当我们取水时，当地人慢慢向我们走近，但当我们派两个人去见他们时，他们又躲得远远的了。

他们远远地看着我们，这样才觉得安全。过了一会儿，他们把独木舟聚到一起，把它们推到浪尖，又带着另外两条船走了。我们走到房子前，发现礼物还是扔在地上时的样子。

4月30日，星期一：我们跟当地居民碰面越来越频繁，但没有真正接触过。他们想要通过叫喊和炫耀武器来吓跑我们。好像我们怎么做都没法

---

approach *v.* 靠近；接近　　　　　　encounter *n.* 偶然碰到；遇见

ADVENTURE TRIP II

mean no harm.

Tuesday, May 1: Ten of us went ashore today, including the Captain, Dr. Solander, and Mr. Banks. We resolved to walk until we were *exhausted*, to see as much as possible. Much of the land is either swampy or sandy soil. Few species of trees, and a lot of grasses. We passed many native houses, all empty, and left beads and ribbons in each. We saw an animal about as tall as a young man, which looked like a rat that stood on its hind legs. It had a large tail that it used to support its weight as it stood. We also saw tracks of a creature about the size of a *weasel* and tracks of a wolf-like creature.

让他们相信我们绝无恶意。

5月1日，星期二：今天我们又有10个人上岸，包括船长、索兰德医生和班克斯先生。为了能尽可能多地了解这里，我们决定一直走，走到筋疲力尽。这里大部分土壤不是沼泽就是沙地。树木种类极少，却不乏草地。我们路过很多当地的人家，房子全是空的，每间房子里都有扔下的玻璃珠和丝带。我们看到一个有一人高的动物，看上去就像一只靠后腿站立的老鼠。它有一只大尾巴，可以支撑着身体站立。我们还看到一串像鼬鼠那么大的动物的脚印，还有类似狼的生物留下的脚印。

---

exhausted adj. 筋疲力尽的   weasel n. 鼬鼠

◆ THE REEF

Friday, May 4: I had each of the last two days off from serving Mr. Banks. Wednesday was rainy and yesterday he devoted to *cataloguing* plant samples. I spent time with other members of the crew. We caught a variety of fish that were well enjoyed for dinner. We also collected many *berries* of the Jambosa variety, much like a cherry, but not as sweet. We ate as many of the berries as we could pick and took more back to the crew on board ship.

Sunday, May 6: We are back to the ocean today. We hear the mapping of the coast is going well.

5月4日，星期五：最近两天我都没有去协助班克斯先生。星期三下雨，昨天他又一直忙于给植物样本做目录分类。我跟其他船员待在一起，抓了各种杂鱼，享受了一顿美味的晚餐。我们也采摘了很多蒲桃品种的浆果，很像樱桃，但没樱桃那么甜。我们摘了很多浆果，吃了个尽兴，还给在船上的船员们带回去好多。

5月6日，星期日：今天我们回到海上，听说绘制沿海地图进展得很顺利。

---

catalogue *v.* 编入目录　　　　　　　　　　　　　　　　　　**berry** *n.* 浆果

ADVENTURE TRIP II

This afternoon we burned some gunpowder in the hold to clean the air. The Captain then ordered us to build a fire in an iron pot to dry the area. Don't know that it works, but the gunpowder and smoke smell better than the usual *stench*.

I had only one shift on deck today. I was quite without amusement for much of the day. I wrote another letter to my daughter, Chelsey.

Sunday, May 20: As we have moved away from shore, we have encountered a reef where the water is very shallow. The captain has told everyone to be alert for it, and to yell warning if we see it in our path. The water is very clear and we can see the color of sand on the bottom with no trouble. We also have a fine view of creatures

---

下午，我们在船舱中烧了些火药来净化空气，然后船长让我们在铁锅里烧火来使这里干燥一些。虽然不知道会不会有效果，不过火药味和烟味总好过往日的臭气熏天吧。

今天在甲板上我只需要换一次班，这一天剩下的时间我感到百无聊赖。于是我又给女儿切尔西写了另外一封信。

5月20日，星期日：就在我们要离岸时，在浅水区碰到一个暗礁。船长提醒大家要提高警惕，如果我们在航线上看到暗礁一定要大喊示警。海水很清澈，我们一眼就能看到海底沙子的颜色。在船周围游来游去的各种生物也让我们大饱眼福，我们看到了几只鲨鱼、海豚、很多鱼，还有一只

---

stench *n.* 臭气；恶臭

◆ THE REEF

swimming around the ship, including several sharks, dolphins, many fish, and a large turtle.

Monday, May 21: Quiet day, little to report. We dropped anchor tonight at 8 to avoid drifting toward the reef in the darkness.

Tuesday, May 22: Dropped anchor in a large bay this evening, *resolved* to go ashore tomorrow in search of plants.

Saturday, May 26: We found ourselves in a channel between two strips of land. The water became very shallow and we dropped anchor to check things over. We set afloat in two of the small boats to *scout* a passage.

Sunday, May 27: The boats returned today with word that there is

大海龟。

　　5月21日，星期一：很平静的一天，没有什么需要记的。为了避免黑暗中碰到暗礁，我们晚上8点就抛锚了。

　　5月22日，星期二：晚上在一个大海湾抛了锚，决定明天到岸上寻找植物。

　　5月26日，星期六：我们发现自己在两片狭长陆地形成的海峡中。这里的水很浅，我们抛了锚来展开全面勘察。我们放出了两艘小船去探出一条通道。

　　5月27日，星期日：今天去巡视的小船回来了，说里面没有路可以通

resolve *v.* 决定；决心　　　　　　　　　scout *v.* 侦察；搜寻

ADVENTURE TRIP II

no *passage* through and we are to turn back. We retraced our course and again fell in with the main coast.

Tuesday, May 29: Mr. Banks went ashore with the Doctor. My assistance was not needed, so I stayed on board and fished with the crew. We caught several large fish and many smaller ones.

Wednesday, May 30: Went ashore looking for fresh water today. No luck. It seems this land is subject to a severe rainy season, and this is not that season.

Thursday, May 31: Because of the number of *sandbars* and *shoals*, we have sent the longboat, The Pinnacle, ahead to scout a route. We will continue to drop anchor each night.

过，我们得往回走。我们折回到我们的航线，又回到了主海岸。

5月29日，星期二：班克斯先生跟医生上了岸。他不需要我的协助，所以我留在船上，跟船员们钓鱼。我们钓到了几只大鱼和很多小鱼。

5月30日，星期三：今天去岸上寻找淡水。可惜没找到。此地似乎经常受到严重的雨季的影响，不过现在不是雨季。

5月31日，星期四：由于沿途有大量的沙洲和浅滩，我们派大划艇"山巅之船"前去探路。每天晚上就照常抛锚。

---

passage *n.* 通路　　　　　　　　　　　　　　sandbar *n.* 沙洲
shoal *n.* 浅滩

◆ THE REEF

Friday, June 1: A crewman today complained about *swollen gums*. He said they had been bothering him for a fortnight, but not knowing the cause, he said nothing. The doctor prescribed lemon juice in all his drinks.

Friday, June 8: We went ashore yesterday thinking we had spotted *coconut* trees, but we were wrong. Mr. Banks did collect some more plant samples.

We continue to sail between the mainland and several small islands and shoals. The anchor is dropped most nights, which is slowing our progress.

Sunday, June 10: Captain Cook has been hugging the coastline

6月1日，星期五：今天一个船员抱怨牙龈肿痛。他说已经疼了两个星期了，不过不知道病因，所以之前并没有提及此事。医生嘱咐他在所有饮品中都添加柠檬汁。

6月8号，星期五：昨天我们以为看到了椰子树，上岸后发现看错了。班克斯先生收集到了更多的植物样本。

我们继续在大陆、几座小岛和浅滩之间航行。我们几乎每晚都抛锚，这阻碍了我们前行的速度。

6月10日，星期日：我们继续向北走，库克船长一直让我们沿着海岸

swollen *adj.* 肿胀的
coconut *n.* 椰子

gum *n.* 牙龈

ADVENTURE TRIP II

as we move north, trying to avoid the reef and the small islands that we have found. At nightfall we spotted a sandbar ahead and during supper passed over it in about seven fathom (42 feet/13m) of water. The Captain and his *lieutenant* assumed we had passed over the tail end of the shoal and that we could rest easy. We did not drop anchor so as to take advantage of a brisk breeze.

Midnight: We have run *aground*! Maybe an hour ago, or so, the ship got stuck on a reef and we can't get her loose. The Captain ran on deck in his nightclothes. We are firmly stuck. We floated a small boat to check the damage and found ourselves stuck upon a coral reef. This is the worst, as it is sharp and can destroy a ship's hull.

线航行，他想尽力避开我们所发现的暗礁和小岛。黄昏时，我们发现前面有沙洲，晚饭期间我们以吃水7英寻（42英尺/13米）的深度越过了沙洲。船长和上尉以为我们已经穿过了浅滩的末端，这下可以放宽心了。为了借力于轻快的微风，我们没有抛锚。

午夜：我们的船被搁浅了！或许在一个小时之前，轮船就被暗礁卡住了，我们没能把船松动开。船长穿着睡衣跑到了甲板上。船卡得太牢，我们就派了一只小船下去查看受损情况，结果发现船卡在一座珊瑚礁上。这下可惨了，因为珊瑚礁很锋利，它可以破坏整个船体。大概有12条木板脱

---

lieutenant n. 海军上尉　　　　　　　　　　aground adv. 搁浅地

◆ THE REEF

There are maybe 12 wooden strips torn from the ship's false keel floating around the bow of the ship.

The men are afraid the ship is badly damaged, and that we might be stranded here with no way to get home. We had been sailing for at least three or four hours since the sight of land, so we know we are not very close.

The waves are beating us against the reef and we can hear the wood cracking. We are being tossed like a *cork* on the waves, so that we can barely keep our feet beneath us. The tide has *ebbed* and we did not get the anchors dropped as the captain ordered. We will be stuck here for at least 12 hours at the mercy of the waves and the rock.

离了轮船的龙骨护板，漂浮在船头周围。

我们都怕船损坏得太严重，那样我们可能被困在这儿，别想回家了。从看到陆地到现在，我们已经航行了至少三四个小时了，所以我们知道离陆地比较远了。

海浪拍打着我们的船，轮船撞击着珊瑚礁，我们还可以听到木头断裂的噼啪声。我们像是在浪尖被拍打的软木，站都站不稳。等潮水退去，我们照船长的命令，没有抛锚。我们将被困在这里至少12个小时，任凭海浪和岩石的摆布。

---

cork *n.* 软木   ebb *v.* 退潮

ADVENTURE TRIP II

Monday, June 11: We are facing NE but the waves threaten to turn us. The sails are all down on Captain's orders last night. No one slept last night, but the officers are all calm and *rational*.

We will drop anchors off the aft deck near noon to take advantage of the high tide. We hope to drag ourselves free and refloat the ship.

The vessel is heaving and shifting very badly. Water has entered the ship through the damaged hull. The Captain has ordered us to lighten the load. We threw overboard our *ballast*, firewood, some of our stores, our water casks, all our water, and six of our cannons. We have started two of the pumps to working in the hold, trying to lower the water level in there. Everyone is pitching in to work the pumps, including the Captain and the other officers.

6月11日，星期一：我们正朝着东北方向，但强劲的海浪险些迫使我们改向。昨晚我们按照船长的命令把帆全部降了下来。昨夜无人入眠，不过船上的长官们一直很镇静、理智。

中午时分，我们借助满潮的优势，在接近船尾的地方抛了锚。我们想好好放松放松，让船也能慢慢浮起来。

轮船上下左右摇晃得很厉害。海水不断从船体受损的地方涌入船里。船长命令我们减轻负载。我们把压舱物、木柴、一些备用品、水桶、所有的水和六座大炮全都扔到船外。我们开始用两个水泵从船舱抽水，以降低那里的水位。每个人都投入到抽水的工作中，包括船长和其他长官们。

---

rational *adj.* 理智的　　　　　　　　　　ballast *n.* 压舱物

◆ THE REEF

11 o'clock AM: It is nearly high *tide*. I am currently on a rest break from the pumps. Everyone puts in fifteen minutes then rests until it is his turn again. We have kept the water from rising much higher, but not in lowering the level too much.

During low tide the ship settled into the rocks and did not heave so much. But from the front holds we could clearly hear the rock *grating* on the *hull*. There is no doubt it will tear a hole in the ship. We have set all four of the pumps working.

I am sitting on deck, since I am too tired to stand. The men are lowering the anchors. The breeze is blowing south right now, and we have raised the sails, hoping the wind will help drag us free.

上午11:00：将近满潮。我这一轮抽水工作完成，可以稍微休息一下了。我们轮流抽水，每个人每次抽水15分钟。我们只是控制了水位不会上升，但并没有使水位降低很多。

在低潮时，船停靠于岩石间，基本不太颠簸了。但在前舱，我们可以很清晰地听到岩石磨得船体嘎吱作响的声音。这样下去，船肯定会戳出个洞。我们已经把四个水泵都用上了。

我坐在甲板上，累得站不起来。船员们继续把锚降低。现在风向为南，我们扬起船帆，希望能借风力摆脱困境。

---

tide *n.* 潮　　　　　　　　　　　　grate *v.* 发出吱嘎吱嘎的摩擦声
hull *n.* 船体

ADVENTURE TRIP II

It didn't work, again. We are stuck. The night tides are higher and we will have to wait until midnight to try again. This feels hopeless. I am afraid I will never see my wife and daughter again. We might well die here, thousands of miles from our homes and families.

7 o'clock PM: We are taking on water quickly as the tide begins to rise again. One of the four *pumps* has failed and cannot be made to work. The men continue to work in 15-minute shifts, working cheerfully.

Mr. Banks has asked me to help him gather all that we can save and be ready should we need to *abandon* ship. He fears the worst. He mentioned the fear that most of us will be drowned. This might

---

不过还是没有进展，我们仍然卡在那里。晚上潮更高了，我们只能等到半夜再试试看。这一切都让我们感到无望。我恐怕再也见不到我的妻子和女儿了。我们很可能会死在这儿，死在这个离我们家乡和家人数千英里的地方。

下午7:00：我们又要抓紧时间抽水，因为潮水又开始上涨了。有一个水泵失灵不能用了。船员们继续15分钟换一次班儿，干得很起劲儿。

班克斯先生叫我帮他收集所有能留的东西，做好弃船准备。他害怕发生最糟糕的情况，他曾经说过，害怕这样下去我们大部分人都会被淹

---

pump n. 泵   abandon v. 放弃

◆ THE REEF

be a better fate than those who survive might endure. There would be little to live for, stranded so far from home with some of the most *savage* natives on Earth. We would have no way to support ourselves. It might be better to drown.

Evening: The time has come and everyone is very anxious. Fear of death stares us in the face. At 10 o'clock our ship floated and was quickly dragged into deep water. We still can only remove as much water as comes in. Our only hope is to get her into land for repairs as soon as possible or to *salvage* what we can and build a new craft.

Tuesday, June 12: The crew has been working for more than 24 hours and is exhausted. But news came from the hold that we

死。但是被淹死的人却比死里逃生的人更幸福一些。活下来的人生活没有盼头，困在离家千里之外的地方，还要面对地球上的最野蛮的一群土著居民。简直是活不下去，还是被淹死的好。

晚上：又到了涨潮的时间，大家都焦虑不安。每个人的脸上都流露出对死亡的恐惧。10点钟的时候，我们的轮船浮起来了，很快被拖到深水区。我们仍然只能尽力将涌入的水抽出去。我们仅存的希望就是将船拖上陆地修理，或者把船里能用的东西抢出来，再造一艘新船。

6月12日，星期二：船员们已经连续工作超过了24小时，筋疲力尽。

savage adj. 野蛮的   salvage v. 抢救

ADVENTURE TRIP II

are taking in more water than we can pump out. There is four feet of water in the hold. The wind is blowing out to sea so there is no chance of getting ashore any time soon.

The crew dragged in all the small anchors, but had to cut loose one of the small bow anchors, as it is least needed. The men have managed to remove the water from the hold faster than thought, and it was found that the depth was not so much as thought.

One crewman *proposed* a fix that no one has seen used. By using his fix, he said he managed to get home from America with a more badly damaged ship than ours. He was given five men to work on his idea. His fix is to take a smaller, heavy sail and paste it over with a mixture of finely cut rope fiber, wool, and *tar*. The mixture is to be

---

但船舱传来消息说，进来的水比我们抽出去的水还要多。船舱里已有四英尺高的水。风是向着海面吹去的，所以船是没法很快靠岸了。

船员艰难地拉着所有的小锚，但不得不割断其中的一个船首锚，因为它的作用最小。船员们从船舱清除海水的速度比预想的要快些，原来水没有想象的那么深。

一个船员提出一种其他人从未见过的修理方法。他说，他就曾用这种方法修理过一艘比我们这条损毁还严重的船，成功地从美洲回到了家乡。船长派给他五个人，按他的想法修理。他的修理方案是把一个较小的下桅帆和从绳子上剪下来已混合好的纤维物质、羊毛、焦油沥青粘在一起。根

---

propose *v.* 提议　　　　　　　　　　　　　　　　　tar *n.* 焦油；沥青

sunk beneath the ship with the thought that where there is a hole there will be *suction*. One or more of the lumps of the mixture should be sucked into the hole and act as a stop to the water coming in.

The men were so tired that they could no longer keep up with the water entering through the hull. The water was filling the hold again. Everyone was eager to try the fix. In the afternoon it was done and was lowered by ropes, then pulled quickly back against the ship. In about two hours the hold was pumped dry, and to our great surprise, only a small amount of water still leaked in. We went from despair to hope that we could get ashore. We will live.

No matter how dreadful things looked, each man obeyed orders and worked with *enormous* energy. The officers were most *professional*

据哪儿有洞哪儿就会有吸力的理论，将混合物沉到船下。一个或几个这样的混合物就会被破洞吸住，这样就可以防止水进来。

　　船员们都太累了，抽水的速度再也赶不上水涌入船舱的速度了。水又充满了船舱。每个人都热切期望着尝试下那个船员的修理方法。下午，混合物准备好了，我们把那一团东西用绳子沉到海里，然后又迅速提起。大概过了两个小时，船舱的水被抽干了，让我们没想到的是，只有少量的水渗进了船舱。我们从失望中重获希望，这下终于有机会上岸了。我们会活下来的。

　　不管事情看上去有多么可怕，每个人都听从命令，并使出浑身解数完

---

suction *n.* 吸；吸气　　　　　　　　　　enormous *adj.* 极大的
professional *adj.* 职业的

ADVENTURE TRIP II

and calm.

Sunday, June 17: The Captain found a *harbor* in which we might drop anchor and perform repairs. It has everything we need. We cannot believe our luck. The calm weather has kept us out in the bay until today. The crew took *advantage* of this delay to get some much-needed rest. There will be much work to do in the next few days when we enter the harbor.

Friday, June 22: The ship was fully out of water today as the tide fell. We could see the hole was big enough to have sunk a ship with twice our pumps. But by some stroke of luck a piece of coral the size of a large rock had broken off in the hole and slowed the water coming in. It may take many days, but we will be able to *patch* the

成命令。而船上的长官们是最有职业精神、最为沉着冷静的。

6月17日，星期日：船长找了一个海港，我们可以在那里抛锚，进行修理。在那里有我们需要的所有东西。我们不敢相信自己能有这么幸运。无风的天气使我们能够在海湾中一直待到今天。船员们借着这几日的耽搁，充分休息，补充体力。过几天到港后，会有很多工作等着我们去做。

6月22日，星期五：今天，潮水退了，船舱里也完全没有水了。我们看到，就算有八个水泵，那个大洞也足以把船沉下去。但是我们很走运，一块大如岩石的珊瑚礁把洞给补上了，使水流进船的速度慢了下来。修补工作可能需要很多天，但我们终将会补好船，重新出海。

harbor *n.* 海港　　　　　　　　　　**advantage** *n.* 有利条件；优势
patch *v.* 修补

hole and get back to sea.

The Captain has decided that we will return by way of the Cape of Good Hope. There is hope we can find a port to get more *extensive* repairs along the way.

We are not home free, but we are alive to make our way home. I so look forward to seeing my family again.

船长决定借道好望角返航。我们有希望在沿途能找到一个海港，全面修理船只。

虽然回家的路途算不上顺利，但至少我们还能活着回家。我多么期待着再次和家人见面啊！

---

extensive *adj.* 广泛的

ADVENTURE TRIP II

5

The Story of Lewis and Clark I

Two hundred years ago, United States *territory* ended on the east bank of the Mississippi River. Ships had sailed around South America and visited the Pacific coast, but almost nothing was known about the land in between. The French owned the land from the Mississippi River to the Rocky Mountains. Spain *controlled* Texas, the Southwest, and California, and Great Britain controlled Canada.

路易斯和克拉克的故事（一）

200年以前，美国版图只延伸到密西西比河东海岸。在那以前，早已有船只在南美洲航行，并到达了太平洋海岸，但人们却对它们中间的大陆一无所知。法国拥有从密西西比河到落基山的版图，西班牙掌控着田纳西州、美国西南部和加利福尼亚州，大英帝国掌控着加拿大。

---

territory *n.* 领土   control *v.* 控制；管理

◆ THE STORY OF LEWIS AND CLARK I

People in all of these countries believed that there might be a Northwest Passage across North America. They imagined the Northwest Passage as an easy river-going route that would run from the Atlantic to the Pacific. Many people believed that if you sailed all the way up the Missouri River, it would be just a short hike to the top of the Columbia River, where you could sail to the Pacific.

Thomas Jefferson, the country's third *president*, believed that the United States needed to find and control the Northwest Passage if it was going to become a powerful nation. The Northwest Passage would be a great trading route between the nations of North America. Jefferson also loved science, geography, and learning about other cultures. He wanted to send an *expedition* up the

---

所有这些国家的人都认为有一条西北航道穿越北美洲。他们想象着西北航道会是一条易于通行的航线，而这条航线从大西洋指向太平洋。很多人认为，如果沿着密苏里河一直航行下去，不久就会到达哥伦比亚河的上游，从那里就可以航行到太平洋。

美国的第三任总统托马斯·杰弗逊认为，如果美国想成为一个强大的国家就需要找到并控制西北航道。西北航道将成为北美各国间的一条重要贸易航线。杰弗逊热爱科学、地理，还喜欢学习其他国家的文化。他想派一支探险队在密苏里河上航行，沿途记录下西部的动植物，和当地的北美

---

president *n.* 总统　　　　　　　　　　　　expedition *n.* 探险队

ADVENTURE TRIP II

Missouri River. The men would record the plant and animal life of the West, meet with the Native Americans there, and, Jefferson hoped, find the *fabled* Northwest Passage.

Congress set aside $2500 for the expedition, and Jefferson chose his personal *secretary*, Captain Meriwether Lewis, to be its leader. Lewis was a close friend of Jefferson's, and Lewis had spent time in the army in western Pennsylvania and Ohio—which was then the western frontier. Lewis asked his friend William Clark to help him lead the expedition.

Just before Lewis and Clark were set to leave, Jefferson surprised the entire nation. In Europe, France was at war with Great Britain,

---

印第安人见见面，总统更希望他们能找到传说中的西北航线。

国会给这次探险拨款2 500美元，杰弗逊钦定他的私人秘书——海军上校梅里韦瑟·路易斯作为领队。路易斯是杰弗逊亲密的朋友，他还曾在宾夕法尼亚州西部和俄亥俄州的军队服役。那时候，这两个州都是西部的边界。路易斯让他的朋友威廉姆·克拉克帮助他率领探险队。

就在路易斯和克拉克准备出发的时候，杰弗逊总统做出了震惊全国的举动。在欧洲，英法交战，法国的财力迅速消耗。法国人想要卖掉他

---

fabled *adj.* 传说中的   secretary *n.* 秘书

◆ THE STORY OF LEWIS AND CLARK I

and France was losing money fast. The French wanted to sell all of their land in North America. Jefferson bought all 820,000 square miles of land for $15 million dollars—only three cents an acre. This deal, known as "the Louisiana Purchase", almost doubled the size of the United States. Many people *criticized* Jefferson—after all, he had no idea what lay in the land he had just bought. Suddenly, Lewis and Clark's expedition had become much more important. They were now setting out to *explore* the newest part of the United States.

Preparation

In 1803, the year that Jefferson set the expedition in motion,

们在北美的所有土地，杰弗逊花了1 500万美元买下了82万平方英里的土地——平均每英里只花了3美分。这笔交易史称"路易斯安那购买案"，几乎把美国的领土扩大了一倍。很多人批评杰弗逊；毕竟他并不知道他刚买下的土地上有些什么。这样一来，路易斯和克拉克的探险就变得更加重要了。他们现在准备出发，去探索美国刚刚买下的那片土地。

出发前的准备

杰弗逊总统在1803年派出了探险队穿越北美，这一举动在当时看来

criticize v. 批评   explore v. 探险

ADVENTURE TRIP II

crossing North America was as challenging and mysterious as traveling to the moon. No one knew what lay between the Mississippi and the Pacific Ocean—there were rumors that woolly *mammoths* still roamed the nation. Most Americans thought that the Native Americans were *hostile* and dangerous. Without cars, telephones, maps, or modern medicine, the journey was sure to be dangerous. Lewis and Clark were risking their lives. Luckily, Lewis was a thoughtful planner.

Lewis traveled to Philadelphia to learn mapmaking, *navigation*, plant and animal identification, and other necessary skills. He bought everything the explorers would need for the trip. He purchased tons

---

如同人类登上月球一样具有挑战性和神秘性。没有人知道密西西比河与太平洋之间到底有什么——有传言说长着毛的猛犸象还活跃在那片土地上。多数美国人认为那里的印第安土著人很危险，对外来者有敌意。没有汽车、电话、地图和先进的药物，旅途注定充满危险。路易斯和克拉克是冒着生命危险去探险的。幸运的是，路易斯是一个思维缜密的策划者。

路易斯去费城学习制作地图、航海、动植物鉴定和其他的必需技能。他买了旅途所需的一切东西，露营用品就有好几吨，包括短柄小斧、鱼

---

mammoth *n.* 猛犸（象）   hostile *adj.* 怀敌意的
navigation *n.* 航行

of camping supplies, including *hatchets*, fishhooks, warm clothing, and material for tents. He also bought hundreds of pounds of dried corn, salted pork, flour, sugar, and 200 pounds of a dried soup mixture called "portable soup". Even with all this food, Lewis and Clark knew that they would have to hunt to get enough to eat. Lewis bought *rifles*, bullets, and barrels of gunpowder. The barrels were made of lead, which could be melted and formed into bullets when the bullets ran out.

Lewis also bought hundreds of dollars worth of gifts to give to the Native Americans they would meet along the trip. He bought mirrors, *sewing* needles, combs, bright cloth, tobacco, and other hard-to-

钩、保暖衣物和搭帐篷所需的材料。他还买了好几百磅干玉米、咸肉、面粉、糖，还有200磅的固体汤料混合物——"速溶汤"。路易斯和克拉克知道即使带了这么多食物也是不够的，他们仍需要通过捕猎获得足够的食物。路易斯买了步枪、子弹和火药筒。火药筒是用铅做成的。当子弹用完时，火药筒就可以熔化掉，做成子弹。

路易斯还买了价值几百美元的礼物赠送给路上碰到的印第安土著人。他买了镜子、缝纫针、梳子、鲜艳的布料、烟草，还有其他很难制造的东

---

hatchet *n.* 短柄小斧   rifle *n.* 步枪
sewing *n.* 缝纫

ADVENTURE TRIP II

make goods. The gifts would show the Native Americans that the Lewis and Clark expedition came in peace. Lewis also arranged for three boats that would take them up the Missouri River. A 55-foot keelboat would carry men and their supplies, and two smaller *canoes* would be useful for scouting ahead.

Lewis and Clark made sure that they chose the best people to make the trip with them. They chose mostly young men, many of whom had been in the army. Some were excellent at boating, while others were good hunters. They chose some men who knew how to fix rifles and some who could use iron to make *horseshoes*, axes, and

西。这些礼物会向印第安土著人表明他们此行绝无恶意。路易斯还安排了三只船带他们驶过密苏里河。一只55英尺长的船是载人和必需品的，另两只小一些的独木舟是用来在前方勘探的。

路易斯和克拉克挑选了他们认为最优秀的人和他们一起出行。他们主要选择年轻人，其中多数在军队中服过役。一些人非常擅长驶船，一些人擅长狩猎。他们挑选了一些会修理步枪的和会用铁做马掌、斧子等必备工具的人，还选了会说土著语言的人。其中一个人是克拉克的非裔美国奴

---

canoe *n.* 独木舟   horseshoe *n.* 马掌

other necessary tools. They also chose men who could speak Native American languages. One member of the team was William Clark's African-American slave, York. The 45 men who eventually set out on the journey became known as the Corps (KORE) of Discovery.

Lewis and Clark brought all of their supplies to St. Louis, near where the Missouri River joins the Mississippi. The Corps of Discovery rowed up the Mississippi to set up camp for the winter of 1803. There, on the edge of unknown land, the men trained for their journey, making sure that they worked well together both *physically* and *mentally*. After waiting out the winter, the Corps of Discovery finally set off up the Missouri River on May 14, 1804.

隶，名叫约克。这45个人终于踏上了被后人称为"探险部队"的旅程。

路易斯和克拉克把所有的必需品都带到了圣路易斯——即靠近密苏里河与密西西比河交汇的地方。1803年，"探险部队"划到了密西西比河沿岸露营过冬。在那片近乎未知的土地上，路易斯和克拉克为了这次旅行训练着他们的部队，以确保他们无论是行动上还是心理上都能很好地合作。"探险部队"在等待中度过了冬天，终于在1804年5月14号从密苏里河上出发了。

physically *adv.* 身体上   mentally *adv.* 精神上；思想上

ADVENTURE TRIP II

Going Upriver

The Missouri River has the nickname "Big Muddy", and Lewis and Clark soon found out why. The river was wide, full of curves, and not very deep. It was often filled with floating wood and dead trees. The thick, muddy water made these hazards hard to see. The Corps was also moving against the strong current, so they went extremely slowly. When the water was deep enough, the men used poles, oars, or sails (if the wind was good) to move *upstream*. But the boats often got caught on the river bottom, forcing the men to get out and drag the boats along using ropes. If that were not enough, the soft, sandy banks of the river often *collapsed* suddenly—at one point, a collapse

---

向上游行进

密苏里河有一个昵称叫作"大泥巴",路易斯和克拉克很快就明白了为什么这么叫它。河面很宽,河道曲折,但河水不深。河面上总是漂满了浮木和枯树,厚厚堆积着的泥土使探险队很难看到这些危险,再加上还要和强劲的激流做斗争,所以他们行进得极其缓慢。当水足够深的时候,他们就用杆、浆,或者是帆(当风力够足的时候)逆流行驶。但是船经常卡在河底,队员们就必须下船来用绳子拉船。有时情况会更加糟糕,柔软多

---

upstream *adv.* 逆流地   collapse *v.* 坍塌

◆ THE STORY OF LEWIS AND CLARK I

ADVENTURE TRIP II

almost sank the keelboat.

The only thing the men had to drink was *muddy* river water, which often made them sick. Hard work gave them *blisters*, boils, upset stomachs, and muscle strains. Lewis had learned a little bit about medicine while he was in Philadelphia, but in 1804, medicine often did more harm than good. The men had no way to ease their pain or keep their wounds clean, and they were in *constant* discomfort. Every man who kept a journal wrote about the horrible mosquitoes. Sudden *hailstorms* cut and bruised the explorers. Wind and rain drove them back down the river. The adventure seemed more like a punishment.

沙的河岸会突然塌陷，这种塌陷有时会导致船沉下去。

他们唯一能喝的东西就是浑浊的河水，因此他们经常生病。繁重的工作使他们起了水疱，生了疮，还受到反胃和肌肉拉伤的折磨。在费城的时候，路易斯学了一点医学知识，但是在1804年，药物治疗通常会使情况变得更糟。队员们没有办法减轻痛苦，也不能保持伤口清洁，所以他们的身体状况一直很差。每个记日记的人都记录着蚊子有多么可怕，还有突降的雹暴淋得他们浑身瘀青。暴风骤雨一次次将船队冲向河的下游。这不太像一次探险，倒像是一场惩罚。

---

muddy *adj.* 浑浊的
constant *adj.* 连续发生的；不断的

blister *n.* 水疱
hailstorm *n.* 雹暴

◆ THE STORY OF LEWIS AND CLARK I

After two months, the men had not made it out of the modern state of Missouri. As the summer wore on, one of the men, Sergeant Charles Floyd, grew ill. On August 20th, he died, probably of a *ruptured* appendix. The Corps buried him in what is now Sioux City, Iowa. *Miraculously*, he was the only member of the expedition to die on the trip.

Into the Plains

Eventually, the land around the Missouri River began to change. The hills gave way to broad plains. There were very few trees, except right along the riverbank. The men began to see *immense* herds

---

两个月过去了，他们还没有走出（今天的）密苏里州。夏天渐渐过去，其中一个叫查尔斯·弗洛伊德的中士病倒了。8月20号，他去世了，可能是阑尾破裂导致的。大家把他埋在了现在的艾奥瓦州苏城。很难得的是，在这次探险中，只有他一人不幸身亡。

到达平原

最终，密苏里河周边的土地开始有了变化。大山变成了辽阔的平原，只有岸边才有树木。他们能看到大群大群的野牛，有时能有几千头。杰弗

---

rupture *v.* 破裂；断裂 　　miraculously *adv.* 奇迹般地
immense *adj.* 巨大的

ADVENTURE TRIP II

of bison, sometimes numbering thousands of animals. President Jefferson had instructed all of the men to take note of any new plants and animals they discovered. The men described pronghorn *antelope*, jackrabbits, prairie dogs, and coyotes, all of which were unknown in the East.

The Lewis and Clark expedition had entered the Great Plains. At the time, these plains were one of the largest grasslands in the entire world. They must have looked much like the African Serengeti Plains you see in nature films today. They seemed endless, *uninhabited*, and filled with wildlife.

The men's journals were filled with descriptions of new

逊总统指示过所有的人都要记下发现的新的动植物，队员们描述了叉角羚、长耳大野兔、草原犬鼠和草原狼的样子，而这些动物在东部根本就没人知道。

路易斯和克拉克的探险队已经进入了大平原。当时，这个平原是全世界最大的草原之一，看起来很像今天我们在自然纪录片中看到的非洲塞伦盖蒂平原。平原一望无际，人迹罕至，到处都是野生动物。

探险队员们的日志中记满了对于新发现的描述，狩猎相当有趣。当杀

---

antelope *n.* 羚羊　　　　　　　　　　　uninhabited *adj.* 无人居住的

◆ THE STORY OF LEWIS AND CLARK I

discoveries, and the hunting was excellent. When they killed an animal, they preserved its *skeleton* and hide in a crate, which they planned to send back to President Jefferson in Washington.

But the plains were not uninhabited. Native Americans had been living and hunting there for thousands of years. Lewis and Clark's expedition did not see many of them at first, because many of the tribes were nomadic, or moved from place to place with no *permanent* home.

Eventually, the Corps of Discovery came into contact with *representatives* of the Missouri, Yankton Sioux, and Lakota tribes.

掉一个动物以后，他们留下其骨架然后藏入大木箱里，打算把这些东西带回去给在华盛顿的杰弗逊总统看。

但是平原并不是无人居住的，印第安土著人已经在那里生活、狩猎了几千年了。在开始的时候，队员们并没有看到很多土著人，因为很多部落都过着游牧生活——他们总是移居，没有固定的家园。

最后，探险部队与密苏里杨克顿苏族和拉克塔族部落的代表进行接触。多数土著人欢迎探险队的到来并接受了他们象征和平的礼物。很多人

---

skeleton *n.* 骨架
representative *n.* 代表

permanent *adj.* 永久的

ADVENTURE TRIP II

Most Native Americans welcomed the explorers and accepted their gifts of peace. Many of them were *fascinated* by York, the African-American slave. Most Native Americans had seen or heard of white people, but they had never seen an African-American. One elderly Native American even rubbed York's skin, thinking he was a white man who had painted himself to trick them. York had fun with the attention. He played games with the children and showed off.

In September, the expedition met with the Lakota, an extremely powerful tribe that controlled most of the trade along the lower Missouri River. The Lakota did not like the idea that another nation now controlled their land and would soon be taking over the river.

都对非裔奴隶约克感兴趣。其实，有很多土著人见过或是听说过白人，但却没见过非裔美国人。一个年长的土著人甚至去蹭约克的皮肤，以为他是一个把自己涂上颜色的白人，想和他们开玩笑。约克很喜欢这种被关注的感觉，他和孩子们做游戏，还不时炫耀着自己。

九月，探险队见到了一个极其有权力的部落——拉克塔族，他们控制着密苏里河下游的大部分贸易。他们不喜欢另一个民族控制他们的土地，而且还要掌管这条河流。路易斯和克拉克总是在土著人中做演讲，称他们为"孩子"，说在东部他们有一个新的"伟大的白人父亲"，但拉克塔族

---

fascinate *v.* 吸引

◆ THE STORY OF LEWIS AND CLARK I

Lewis and Clark often made speeches to the Native Americans, calling them "children", and saying that they had a new "great White father" in the east. The Lakota did not like being called "children".

When Lewis and Clark sailed into Lakota territory in what is now South Dakota, there was *tension* in the air. The Lakota were not satisfied by Lewis and Clark's gifts. Some of the Lakota grabbed hold of one of the pirogues. Lewis, who had a hot temper, got into an argument with the chiefs. But luckily, Clark, who was more even-tempered, and a Lakota chief, Black Buffalo, calmed everyone down. The expedition continued safely.

As fall approached, the weather began to grow colder. Light

人不喜欢被称作"孩子"。

当路易斯和克拉克驾船驶入拉克塔族的领地时（也就是现在的南达科他州），空气里有一种紧张的气氛。他们对路易斯和克拉克的礼物并不满意。一些族人控制住了他们其中一条船，路易斯脾气暴躁，和首领吵了起来。幸亏性情温和的克拉克和拉克塔族的一个首领布莱克·巴弗洛，才把争吵平息了下来。探险才得以平安地继续。

秋天快到的时候，天气转凉。早在十月份，就飘起了清雪，天空中

---

tension *n.* 紧张

ADVENTURE TRIP II

snow began to fall as early as October, and flocks of geese filled the sky, heading south for the winter. The expedition came upon a town of Mandan Native Americans, who lived in *sturdy* sod houses. The Mandan were friendly and welcoming. Lewis and Clark realized that they would not reach the end of the Missouri River before winter. They decided that the Mandan town would be a good place to make camp until spring.

Spending the Winter

The Corps of Discovery built a sturdy *fort* near the Mandan town and made friends with the Native Americans. The explorers were lucky that they got along so well with the Native Americans, because the weather quickly turned harsh. Most of the men had grown up in

---

大雁成群，飞到南方去过冬了。探险队来到了曼丹族土著人的一个镇上，曼丹族人住在坚固的草泥墙房子里，他们友好、热情。路易斯和克拉克知道，他们即使继续前行，走出密苏里河时也是冬天了。他们决定在曼丹镇安营扎寨，春天再动身。曼丹镇是个不错的地方。

度过冬天

"探险部队"在曼丹城附近建造了一个坚固的堡垒，并和当地的土著人成了朋友。严寒很快来临了，队员们觉得很幸运，能和土著人相处得那

---

sturdy *adj.* 结实的；坚固的   fort *n.* 堡垒

Virginia, and they were totally unfamiliar with the difficult winters of the northern plains. They traded with the Native Americans to get food, tools, and warm bedding. Lewis also offered his medical skills to the Mandan. On one extremely cold February night, he was asked to help *deliver* a baby.

The woman who was giving birth was Sacagawea, the wife of a French Canadian fur trapper. She was a member of the Shoshone tribe, who lived near the source of the Missouri River. Lewis thought that she could be an excellent guide and *interpreter* on their journey. The baby was born safely, and the mother and her infant son joined Lewis and Clark's Corps of Discovery.

么好。大多数队员都是在弗吉尼亚长大的，他们根本就不知道北方平原的冬天是多么冷。他们向印第安土著人换取食物、工具和温暖的被子。路易斯还为曼丹族人治病。在二月份一个非常寒冷的夜晚，他被叫去接生。

即将生产的那个女人叫萨卡加维亚，她是一个法裔加拿大毛皮猎人的妻子。她是肖松尼部落的成员，这个部落住在密苏里河源头的附近。路易斯觉得，萨卡加维亚很适合做他们旅途中的向导和翻译。等到孩子平安地出生后，这对母子就加入了路易斯和克拉克的"探险部队"。

---

deliver *v.* 接生；助产   interpreter *n.* 口译译员

ADVENTURE TRIP II

◆ THE STORY OF LEWIS AND CLARK I

The winter of 1804 and 1805 was very harsh. Food ran low. By springtime, the Corps of Discovery was eager to be on the move again. The Native Americans told them of a large waterfall not far upstream. Lewis and Clark believed that this *waterfall* was a signal that they were approaching the Continental Divide, where the rivers begin flowing west, toward the Pacific Ocean. The Corps of Discovery was sure that the Northwest Passage was not far off.

On April 7, 1805, the Corps of Discovery headed west once more with hope in their hearts.

1804年和1805年的冬天异常严酷，食物短缺。到了春天，"探险部队"期盼着再次动身。印第安土著人告诉他们，在上游附近有一个很大的瀑布。路易斯和克拉克认为，瀑布标志着他们正在接近洛杉矶山脉分水岭，水从那里开始向西流入太平洋。"探险部队"确信西北航道就在不远处。

1805年4月7号，"探险部队"满怀希望，再次向西行进。

waterfall *n.* 瀑布

ADVENTURE TRIP II

6

The Story of Lewis and Clark II

On May 14, 1804, Captains Meriwether Lewis and William Clark headed up the Missouri River with their group, the Corps (KOR) of Discovery. They hoped to find an easy way to travel on rivers from the Atlantic Ocean to the Pacific. This route, called the Northwest Passage, would open up the vast new territory of the United States for *traders* and settlers.

By the spring of 1805, they had traveled 1,500 miles (2,400

路易斯与克拉克的故事(二)

1804年5月14日,梅里韦瑟·路易斯船长与威廉·克拉克船长率领"探险部队"朝着密苏里河进发,希望能找到一条从大西洋到太平洋的便捷水道。这条水道,也称西北航道,将在商人和当地居民眼前展开一片崭新的美国大陆。

到1805年春天,船队已经航行了1 500英里(约合2 400公里)了。

---

trader *n.* 商人

km), met many Native American tribes, lost one explorer to illness, and spent a *freezing* winter in a fort they built themselves. Now, it was time to head out again. Over the winter, three new people joined the expedition: a French fur trapper, his young Shoshone wife, Sacagawea, and their infant son, Jean-Baptiste, who Clark nicknamed "Little Pomp". On April 7, 1805, the Corps of Discovery launched its boats and headed west again.

The Fork and the Falls

The wildlife around the Missouri River continued to *astound* Lewis and Clark. Bison, elk, grizzly bears, and antelope covered the plains.

他们遇到了许多土著部落。一名探险队员因病死亡；他们还在一处自行搭建的堡垒中度过了一个寒冬。现在，该重新起航了。冬天过后，有三位新人加入了探险：一位法国毛皮猎人，猎人年轻的肖松尼族的妻子萨卡加维亚，还有他们的幼子让·巴蒂斯特。克拉克给这孩子起了个小名，叫"小邦普"。1805年4月7日，探险部队再次向西航行。

岔口与瀑布

密苏里河沿岸的野生动植物仍然让路易斯和克拉克吃惊不已。平原上到处都是美洲野牛、麋鹿、灰熊和羚羊。狩猎往往收获颇丰；探险者们喜

---

freezing *adj.* 极冷的　　　　　　　　　　　astound *v.* 使震惊

ADVENTURE TRIP II

The hunting was good; the explorers grew fond of roasted beaver tail while Sacagawea helped them find wild artichokes, turnips, berries, and herbs. Soon they saw beautiful *limestone* formations rising along the riverbanks. The team was sure it was coming close to the place where the Missouri River ended and the Columbia River began. Everything seemed to be going perfectly.

On June 2, the boats came to a fork in the river. None of the Native Americans had *mentioned* this fork, and nobody knew which way to take. Captain Lewis and Captain Clark split up, and each took a group to explore one branch of the river. Most of the explorers were sure that the north fork was the real Missouri. But the captains believed the south fork was correct. Captain Lewis took a second

---

欢吃烤海狸尾巴，萨卡加维亚则帮他们寻些野洋蓟、芜菁、浆果，或者香草。很快，他们发现了沿着河堤长起来的美丽的石灰岩层。探险队确信，他们已经快到密苏里河的尽头和哥伦比亚河发起的交界处了。看起来一切都非常顺利。

6月2日，船队来到了一处岔口。所有的土著人都没有提到过这个岔口，谁也不知道该走哪条路。路易斯船长和克拉克船长分开走，各自带领一支队伍去探索这两条支流。探险者们大多认为北向的岔口才是密苏里河，但两位船长却认为是南向那条。路易斯船长又一次向南边的岔口航

---

limestone *n.* 石灰石   mention *v.* 提到

◆ THE STORY OF LEWIS AND CLARK II

trip up the south fork, where he heard the roaring of a waterfall. The Native Americans had told him about the Great Falls of the Missouri River. Now he was sure the south fork was correct. Even though most of the team believed that Lewis and Clark were wrong, they followed their trusted leaders.

Lewis and Clark thought it would be easy to carry their boats and supplies around the falls. The group carved wooden wheels to help drag the boats. But they still had to cut a path through the thick cottonwood trees. The ground was covered with *prickly* pear cactus. The *thorns* pierced the team's moccasins. One man was bitten by a rattlesnake, and everyone was *tortured* by the mosquitoes. Lewis had thought it would only take them a few hours to get around the falls.

行，并且听见了瀑布的咆哮声。土著人曾经告诉过他有关密苏里河大瀑布的事儿。而今，他确信南向的支流是正确的。尽管大部分队员认为两位船长是错的，但出于信任，他们还是跟随船长前行。

路易斯与克拉克认为，把船只和物资运到瀑布周围是件容易事儿。为了拉动船只，队员们削制了木轮子，但他们还需要从棉白杨树丛中砍出一条通道来。地上满是带刺的仙人球，它们刺穿了队员们的莫卡辛软皮鞋子。有人被响尾蛇咬到了；所有人都饱受蚊虫叮咬之苦。路易斯以为只要几个小时就能到瀑布脚下，结果队伍走了将近一个月才到。

---

prickly *adj.* 多刺的   thorn *n.* 刺
torture *v.* 使痛苦；使受煎熬

ADVENTURE TRIP II

It took them almost a month.

Finally, they could float their boats on the river again. Sacagawea began to *recognize* the territory of her Shoshone tribe. Lewis and Clark both believed they would soon find the Columbia River, which led west to the Pacific Ocean.

The river *forked* into three branches, and the Corps of Discovery took the west branch. It was only a small creek now. A Native American trail ran alongside the creek and up a ridge. Lewis leapt onto the trail. He was sure that at the top, he would see the Columbia River, and possibly even a great plain leading to the Pacific Ocean. Finally, he reached the top of the ridge.

最后，他们的船终于能够重新下水了。萨卡加维亚认出了肖松尼族的领地。路易斯和克拉克都相信，他们很快就能找到哥伦比亚河，只要一路向西就能抵达太平洋。

河流岔出三条分支，"探险部队"走了向西的那一支。现在那里只是一条小河，一条土著人踏出的小道沿着小河通向山脊。路易斯三步并作两步走上小道。他确信能在山顶望见哥伦比亚河，甚至还可能看到通向太平洋的大平原。终于，他到达了山脊的最高处。

---

recognize *v.* 认出　　　　　　　　　　　　　　　　fork *v.* 分岔

◆ THE STORY OF LEWIS AND CLARK II

ADVENTURE TRIP II

What he saw astounded him—there was no river, no great plain, and certainly no Pacific Ocean. Instead, he saw mountains. The mountains were taller, wider, and more *impassable* than any mountains he had ever seen. Even though it was early summer, the peaks shone with snow. These were the enormous Rocky Mountains. In that *instant*, Lewis knew that there was no Northwest Passage. But still, he was determined to find a way to the Pacific Ocean, whether it was easy or not.

Over the Mountains

Lewis and Clark knew that they would not be able to take the boats over the Rocky Mountains. Instead, they hoped that

---

令他吃惊的是，那里没有河流，也没有大平原，当然也没有太平洋。他看到的是山脉。那山脉比他见过的任何山脉都更高大、更广袤、更无路可通。虽然当时已是初夏，山峰却仍然闪耀着雪光。这就是壮阔的落基山脉。在那一瞬间，路易斯明白了，根本就没有西北航道。但是，他还是决心找到通往太平洋的路，在所不惜。

翻山越岭

路易斯和克拉克明白，他们无法带船翻越落基山脉。他们希望那些肖松尼人，也就是萨卡加维亚的族人，能够把马匹卖给他们。萨卡加维亚来

---

impassable *adj.* 不可通行的　　　　　　　　　　　　　　　　instant *n.* 瞬间

THE STORY OF LEWIS AND CLARK II

the Shoshone, Sacagawea's people, would sell them horses. Sacagawea would be their interpreter and would help *convince* the tribe to sell their horses for the dangerous journey.

Sacagawea was overjoyed to see her tribe again. Another tribe had *kidnapped* her and sold her to her French-Canadian husband when she was only twelve. She had not seen her friends and relatives in years.

Lewis, Clark, and Sacagawea sat down to speak with the chief of the village. Suddenly, Sacagawea leapt up and *embraced* the chief, *sobbing*. The chief was her own brother. The Shoshone agreed to sell the expedition all the horses they needed. They also offered a guide,

---

做他们的翻译，并帮忙说服部落里的人把马卖给他们，他们才能继续危险的旅程。

萨卡加维亚再次见到族人，喜不自胜。另一个部落曾经绑架了她，把她卖给了她的法裔加拿大丈夫，当时她只有12岁。她已经多年没见到朋友和亲人了。

路易斯、克拉克和萨卡加维亚坐下来，与村子里的首领会谈。突然，萨卡加维亚跳起来，呜咽低泣，与首领拥抱在一起。原来这位首领便是她的亲哥哥。肖松尼人同意出售探险所需要的马匹。此外，他们还提供了一

---

convince *v.* 说服；劝说
embrace *v.* 拥抱

kidnap *v.* 绑架
sob *v.* 呜咽

who Lewis and Clark nicknamed Old Toby.

The mountains were tougher than Lewis and Clark ever imagined. The *slopes* were steep and slippery with ice and snow. Men and horses fell and injured themselves. Old Toby could not find the trail among the *snowdrifts* and fallen trees. Each time they came to a ridge, they saw only more mountains. Food was becoming *scarce*, and the team was showing signs of *malnutrition*. Finally, they decided that they had to shoot and eat a horse in order to survive.

The members of the Corps of Discovery were nearly dead when they finally found their way out of the mountains. They arrived in a Nez Perce Native American village. The Native Americans gave them food and helped them build canoes to travel down the rivers, which

---

位向导，路易斯和克拉克称他为"老托比"。

跨越山脉的艰难远远超出路易斯和克拉克的想象。山坡冰雪覆盖，又陡又滑。人员和马匹经常跌倒，伤痕累累。山上满是积雪和倒下的树木，老托比也找不到路了。他们每次到了山脊，都只看到更多的山。食物开始紧缺，队员们也出现了营养不良的迹象。最后，他们不得不射杀一匹马为食，才得以存活下来。

"探险部队"终于找到出山的路时，队员们已经奄奄一息了。他们到达了内兹佩尔塞土著村庄。土著人给了他们食物，还帮助他们建造独木

---

slope *n.* 山坡　　　　　　　　　　snowdrift *n.* （风吹成的）雪堆
scarce *adj.* 缺乏的；不足的　　　　malnutrition *n.* 营养不良

now flowed west, to the Pacific. They were finally on the last leg of their journey.

The Pacific

The Corps of Discovery traveled quickly, now that it was going with the current instead of against it. There were many rapids and waterfalls. Sometimes the explorers were in such a hurry that they simply *floated* down the rapids, hoping to survive. The high, dry plains suddenly changed to the cool rainforests of the Cascade Mountains.

They were getting closer to the sea—the river began to taste salty and to rise and fall with the tides. The entire group was *eager* to see the ocean. But just as it seemed that Lewis and Clark's group

---

舟，以便他们顺河流航行。这条河向西流去，流入太平洋。他们终于到达了旅途的最后一程。

太平洋

"探险部队"速度飞快，他们现在终于转向顺流行进了。急滩和瀑布都很多，探险者们溜下急滩时会吓得手忙脚乱，希望能活下来。似乎就在一瞬间，高耸干燥的平原变成了喀斯开山凉爽的雨林。

他们离大海越来越近了——河水开始变咸，并随着潮水起伏。全体队员都热切地要见到海洋。但是，就在队伍快要抵达太平洋的时候，一场剧

---

float *v.* 漂浮   eager *adj.* 渴望的

ADVENTURE TRIP II

would reach the Pacific, a fierce storm blew in. Cold rain and huge waves *soaked* the Corps. Once they even had to move their camp in the middle of the night so they would not be washed away by the waves.

When the weather improved, the Corps continued down the river. At last, they saw waves, a beach, and a horizon of water. "Ocian in view," Clark, who was a terrible speller, wrote in his journal. "O! The joy!" The Corps of Discovery had made it to the Pacific Ocean.

Winter on the Coast

The weather was beginning to turn cold, and Lewis and Clark needed a place to spend the winter. They were *currently* camped on the north bank of the Columbia River. The Native Americans had told

---

烈的风暴来袭。冰凉的雨水和强大的波浪冲击着船队。有一次，他们甚至被迫半夜里转移营地，以免被波浪卷走。

　　天气稍微好点，探险队就继续行进。最终，他们看见了波浪、海滩、水平线。"大海尽收眼底，哦，欢呼吧！"白字先生克拉克在日记中写道。"探险部队"终于到达了太平洋。

　　沿岸的冬天

　　天气开始冷起来，路易斯和克拉克需要找一个地方过冬。他们目前扎营在哥伦比亚河的北岸。土著人告诉过他们，南岸要更好些，两位领队决

---

soak v. 浸湿　　　　　　　　　　　　　　　currently adv. 现在；目前

the group that the south bank was better. The leaders decided to let the Corps of Discovery vote. Each member had a vote, including the African-American slave, York, and Sacagawea. This was decades before either African-Americans or women could *legally* vote in the United States. The group voted to move to the south bank.

The Corps built a fort they named Fort Clatsop, after the Native American tribe that lived there. The winter was wet, cold, and *miserable*. It rained almost every day, the food was bad, and many of the men were homesick. Thomas Jefferson had promised that if the Corps of Discovery saw any ships on the Pacific, it could ask for a ride home, and the government would pay. But no ships appeared.

定让"探险部队"的队员们投票。每人都有投票权,包括非裔美国奴隶约克和萨卡加维亚。在美国,非裔美国人和妇女几十年后才可以合法投票。探险队根据投票结果,转移到了南岸。

探险队建了一座堡垒,并根据曾生活在那儿的土著部落的名字,称它为克拉特索普堡。那儿的冬天潮湿、寒冷,天气又恶劣。几乎每天都在下雨,食物无法下咽,很多人开始想家。托马斯·杰弗逊总统曾经承诺,"探险部队"见到任何太平洋上的船只,都可以请求送他们回家,政府支付船费。但一艘船也没有。

---

legally adv. 合法地   miserable adj. 非常难受的

ADVENTURE TRIP II

The team spent its time *preparing* to go home and tell the world what it had done and seen. All the men filled in their journals, adding information about the weather, the land, the people, and the *wildlife*. Clark, who turned out to be a natural mapmaker, drew a map of the territory they had crossed. Other men repaired equipment and prepared supplies for the journey.

By the time spring arrived, the explorers were eager to be moving again. On March 23, 1806, they began traveling east, up the Columbia River.

Heading Home

Canoeing up the Columbia River was very difficult, and the Corps

---

探险队花了很多时间准备返程,并向世界宣告他们的所见所为。所有人都记日记,记录下天气、土地、人文和野生动植物的状况。克拉克俨然天生就会绘制地图,他将队伍经过的地方都绘制成了一张地图。其他的人则修理工具,并准备返航所需要的物品。

春天来临的时候,探险者们都等不及要重新启程了。1806年3月23日,他们沿哥伦比亚河而上,开始向东航行。

回家

乘独木舟上溯哥伦比亚河是非常困难的。"探险部队"很快用独木舟

---

prepare *v.* 准备　　　　　　　　　　　　wildlife *n.* 野生动植物

of Discovery soon traded its canoes for horses. They eventually reached the Nez Perce village where they had stumbled out of the mountains. The mountains were still covered with snow, and the group chose to wait for warmer weather rather than risk death again. But after a month, they grew *impatient* and tried to cross the peaks. They found themselves *struggling* through 12-foot snowdrifts, even though it was mid-June. They turned back.

After another week of waiting, they tried again. It was still difficult, but they succeeded with the help of some Nez Perce guides.

From then on, the Corps would be going with the river, over territory they had crossed before. Lewis and Clark decided that they had time to split up and explore. Clark, Sacagawea, and many

换来了马匹。最后，他们到达了内兹佩尔塞村，从那里跌跌撞撞走出了山脉。山脉仍然积雪覆盖，探险队没有冒死前进，而是等待天气暖和起来。可是，一个月后，他们失去了耐性，尝试越过山峰。尽管这时已经是六月中旬，山上等待他们的却是12英尺厚的积雪，探险队举步维艰。于是他们退了回来。

又等了一周，他们再次尝试出山。此时，出行难度依然很大，但在一些内兹佩尔塞向导的帮助下，他们终于成功越过了山脉。

从那以后，探险队就要沿着河流，穿过他们此前走过的地带。路易斯

---

impatient　*adj.*　不耐烦的　　　　　　　　struggle　*v.*　挣扎；斗争

ADVENTURE TRIP II

members of the Corps headed toward the Yellowstone River, where they had left their boats the summer before.

Lewis and a group of nine men went north, coming close to what is now the Canadian *border*. On July 25, while Lewis and his group slept, a band of Blackfoot Native Americans tried to take their horses and guns. Most of the Native Americans ran off when the men awoke. But one man *stabbed* a Native American, and Lewis shot and killed another.

This was the only *violence* between the Corps of Discovery and any of the Native Americans they met. Lewis and his group hurried on to where the Missouri River met the Yellowstone River. There they met part of Clark's party at a place they named Reunion Point. The

和克拉克认为，他们有足够的时间分头探索。克拉克、萨卡加维亚和许多探险队员朝着黄石河行进。去年夏天，他们的船只就留在了那里。

路易斯带着9人的队伍往北而行，靠近了今天的加拿大边境。7月25日，就在路易斯和队员们睡觉的时候，一伙黑腿族土著试图抢走他们的马匹和枪支。他们被响动惊醒，大多数土著人逃走了。一位队员刺中了一名土著人，路易斯射杀了另一名土著人。

这是"探险部队"与所有遇到的土著人唯一的一次暴力事件。路易斯和队员们加速向密苏里河与黄石河交界处行进。他们在约好的地方见到了克拉克团队的一部分人，此处被他们叫作"汇合处"。然后他们继续驾着

border *n.* 边界　　　　　　　　　　　　　　　stab *v.* 刺
violence *n.* 暴力

◆ THE STORY OF LEWIS AND CLARK II

group hurried on by canoe.

They all soon arrived at the Mandan Native American town where they had spent their first winter. They said goodbye to Sacagawea, her husband, and Jean-Baptiste, who were staying in the village. Another member of the Corps, John Colter, also decided to leave the expedition to join a group of fur trappers.

The rest of the expedition continued down the river toward home. They went *swiftly*, encountering many fur trappers, settlers, and explorers who were following in the expedition's footsteps. At last, they reached St. Louis on September 23, 1806. The Corps of Discovery was *overjoyed*, and so were the people of St. Louis. Many people had assumed that the explorers had died along the journey.

独木舟快速行进。

他们很快便全都抵达了曼丹族人的领地，这正是他们度过第一个冬天的地方。萨卡加维亚和她丈夫要带着让·巴蒂斯特留在村里，探险队和他们告别了。另外一位队员约翰·考尔特也决定离开探险队，参加一支毛皮猎人队伍。

探险队其余的人一路往下游返航。他们快速地航行，遇见了许许多多的毛皮猎人、移民，以及跟随他们脚步的探险者。最后，他们于1806年9月23日抵达了圣路易斯。"探险部队"喜出望外，圣路易斯人民也是如此。许多人原以为这些探险家们已在旅途中丧生。

---

swiftly *adv.* 迅速地

overjoyed *adj.* 狂喜的

ADVENTURE TRIP II

◆ THE STORY OF LEWIS AND CLARK II

Jefferson picks Lewis to head exploration team   April 1803
Louisiana Purchase   July 4, 1803
Corps of Discovery *sets out*   May 14, 1804
Sgt. Charles Floyd dies   August 20, 1804
Corps reaches Mandan town   October 24, 1804
Leaves Mandan town   April 7, 1805
Reaches Great Falls of Missouri   June 13, 1805
Reaches Rocky Mountains   August 31, 1805
Finishes crossing Rocky Mountains   Sep. 22, 1805

1803年4月　杰弗逊总统任命路易斯率队
1803年7月4日　路易斯安娜购买案
1804年5月14日　"探险部队"出发
1804年8月20日　查尔斯·弗洛伊德去世
1804年10月24日　探险队到达了曼丹镇
1805年4月7日　探险队离开曼丹镇
1805年6月13日　到达密苏里河大瀑布
1805年8月31日　到达落基山脉
1805年9月22日　穿越落基山脉

set out　动身；出发

ADVENTURE TRIP II

Corps sights Pacific Ocean	Nov. 7, 1805
Begins return journey	March 23, 1806
Returns to Nez Perce	May 28, 1806
The Corps splits up	July 3, 1806
Joins again at *Reunion* Point	August 12, 1806
Reaches Mandan town again	August 14, 1806
Returns to St. Louis	Sep. 23, 1806

The Effects of the Expedition

Lewis and Clark went to Washington, D.C. to visit President Jefferson and present him with the results of their journey. Jefferson was disappointed that there was no Northwest Passage, but he was *delighted* with what Lewis and Clark had done. He carefully studied their new map. He took the animal hides, horns, and skeletons they

---

1805年11月7日	探险队看到了太平洋
1806年3月23日	开始返程
1806年5月28日	返回内兹佩尔塞
1806年7月3日	探险队分两路行进
1806年8月12日	在汇合处重聚
1806年8月14日	再次到达曼丹镇
1806年9月23日	回到圣路易斯

探险的影响

路易斯和克拉克来到华盛顿特区拜访杰弗逊总统，并向他展示了探险

---

reunion *n.* 重聚　　　　　　　　　　　　delighted *adj.* 高兴的

had collected and displayed them in the White House. He *especially* enjoyed the live groundhog that the Corps had shipped to him.

Captain Lewis was named the governor of the new Louisiana Territory. But Lewis was unhappy in his role. He had financial trouble, and many people noticed that he seemed moody and sad. In 1809, he headed toward Washington, D.C. in hopes that Jefferson could help him with his problems. On his way there on October 11, he committed *suicide* with his pistol.

Captain Clark settled in St. Louis, where he had a career in public service, which included serving as the Superintendent of Indian Affairs. He always tried to help the Native Americans who had helped him on his expedition.

的成果。令杰弗逊失望的是西北航线并不存在，但他为路易斯和克拉克的探险感到开心。他仔细研究了他们的新地图，还把他们收集的兽皮、兽角和骨架送到白宫展览。他尤其喜欢探险队在船上带回来的一只活土拨鼠。

路易斯船长被任命为新路易斯安那领地的州长。不过，路易斯并不喜欢这个职位。他遇到了财政困难，很多人发现他情绪低落，郁郁寡欢。1809年，他动身去往华盛顿特区，希望杰弗逊能帮他走出困境。10月11日，他开枪自杀。

克拉克船长在圣路易斯定居下来。他在当地做公务员，其中包括任管理印第安事务的长官。他始终尽力帮助在他探险途中帮助过他的土著人。

---

especially *adv.* 尤其　　　　　　　　　　　suicide *n.* 自杀

ADVENTURE TRIP II

Lewis and Clark's story has been told in hundreds of books, movies, and poems. Everything from schools to *motels* have been named after the two men. But the most important effect of Lewis and Clark's journey was that they opened the American West to settlers, explorers, *prospectors*, and adventurers. They paved the way for the American farms, factories, and cities that we know today. After the Lewis and Clark expedition, the American West was never the same.

记叙路易斯与克拉克事迹的书籍、电影和诗歌有千百种之多。从学校到汽车旅馆以他们名字来命名的场所包罗万象。但是，路易斯与克拉克的探险最重要的影响就在于他们向移居者、探险家、勘探者和冒险家们打开了美洲西部的大门。有他们当年的探险，才有今天美国的农场、工厂和城市。他们的探险给美国西部带来了翻天覆地的变化。

---

motel n. 汽车旅馆　　　　　　　　　　prospector n. 勘探者

◆ VIKINGS

Vikings

What do you think of when you hear the word Vikings? Do you think of warriors, or do you think of explorers? Do you think of *merchants*, or do you think of poets? Well, the Vikings were all these things, and many others as well-like scientists, farmers, and fishermen. But we tend to only think of them as tough, mean, and strong. They are mostly remembered as the best warriors ever

维京人

当你听到"维京人"这个词的时候,你会想到什么?会想到勇士还是探险家,商人还是诗人?其实,这些答案都对,除此之外,他们还是科学家、农民和渔民。但是我们通常只记得他们是多么坚韧、出色和强健。他们通常是人们记忆中最出色的勇士,因为维京人很少

---

merchant *n.* 商人

ADVENTURE TRIP II

known. The Vikings seldom lost a battle. Still, their greatest *traits* may have been their love of exploration and their courage to face the open ocean.

The Vikings lived about a thousand years ago. They had a spirit for adventure and battle. It was natural that they would gain a reputation as fierce people. They were as harsh and rugged as the coastal lands from which they came—lands such as present day—Norway, Sweden, and Denmark. It was natural that many took to the oceans and became great sailors. Their ships were fast and could carry many warriors. Some of their ships even carried horses. Using their sailing skills, thirst for adventure, and bravery, the Vikings *conquered* many lands.

打败仗。然而，他们最伟大的品质或许是他们对探险的热爱和面对广阔海洋的勇气。

维京人生活在大约一千年以前。由于他们富有冒险和战斗精神，被自然而然地称为勇猛的人。他们与他们所居住的沿海岛屿——像今天的挪威、瑞典和丹麦———一样坚韧和粗犷。在这种环境中，许多人开始在海上航行并成了了不起的水手。他们的船开得很快而且能容纳很多勇士，其中的一些船甚至可以承载马匹。维京人利用他们的航海技术、对冒险的渴望和过人的胆量征服了许多土地。

trait *n.* 特征   conquer *v.* 征服

◆ VIKINGS

Over time, the Vikings' spirit of *exploration* and adventure led them to places all around Europe. It even led them to places no one thought *existed*. The Vikings of Denmark headed south. They seized land along the western coast of Europe. They even conquered land along the Mediterranean Sea. The Vikings of Sweden headed into Eastern Europe. And the Vikings of Norway headed west. In fact, Vikings from Norway went as far as North America. And they did so long before Christopher Columbus was even born.

Viking History

We often think of a Viking as a tall, *muscular*, blond man. He might

---

随着时间的推移，维京人探索和冒险的精神指引着他们到达欧洲的各地。这种精神甚至指引他们去探索那些无人知晓的地方。丹麦的维京人向南进发，他们夺取了欧洲西海岸的土地，甚至征服了地中海沿岸的土地。瑞典的维京人进入东欧，挪威的维京人向西扩张。实际上，挪威的那批维京人一直走到了北美洲，也就是说在克里斯托弗·哥伦布出生之前很多年，他们就已经到达了北美洲。

维京人的历史

我们常常把维京人想象成高大、强健、金发的人，他们可能看起来

---

exploration *n.* 探索　　　　　　　　　　　exist *v.* 存在
muscular *adj.* 强壮的

ADVENTURE TRIP II

look like a sturdy, well built wrestler. Our image of Vikings often includes the metal helmet with a horn on each side. In fact, Viking *helmets* were decorated but most likely did not have horns on them.

Most of what we know about the Vikings comes from the people they defeated. These views aren't always accurate. It's hard to be fair when writing about the people who just beat you up, took your money, and burned down your house. And who wants to say they were *defeated* by a bunch of puny guys who don't fight very well? So it is possible that the *historic* images of Vikings were a bit distorted.

It also seems fair to say that the stories told by the Vikings

健壮得像优秀的摔跤运动员。我们想象中的维京人还经常带着有两个角的金属头盔。事实上，维京人的头盔都进行过装饰，但是大部分上面都没有角。

大部分我们所知道的关于维京人的故事都是那些被他们打败的人告诉我们的，所以那些说法不一定都是正确的。当你描写一个人，尤其是刚痛打过你一顿、抢走你的钱还烧毁了你的房子的人时，你很难公平客观地去描写他。并且谁会愿意去说自己是被一群不会打架、微不足道的人打败的呢？所以维京人的历史形象很可能会有一些脱离事实。

很公平地说，维京人自己所叙述的故事也可能会或多或少地夸大事

helmet *n.* 头盔
historic *adj.* 历史上重要的

defeat *v.* 击败

◆ VIKINGS

ADVENTURE TRIP II

themselves are a bit larger than life. Like most warriors, the Vikings liked to talk about their feats. They often sat around celebrating after a battle. They shared stories of their bravery and fighting skills. Like many war stories, the truth became more and more stretched each time stories were told.

In Viking culture, land was handed down from father to his first-born son. Younger sons were given no land. They could either work for the oldest brother or strike out on their own to seek fame and fortune elsewhere. The *rumors* of easy riches won in battle spread quickly. Most young men were well trained as warriors. It seemed natural to strike out for better *opportunity* by conquering other lands.

实。维京人像大多数勇士一样，喜欢讲述他们的功勋。一场战争之后，他们经常围坐在一起庆祝胜利，分享他们英勇的故事和战斗的本领。像许多战争故事一样，真相随着故事一次次的讲述而不断被夸大。

在维京人的文化中，土地要从父辈传给第一个出生的儿子，其他的孩子都没有土地。他们可以选择给年长的哥哥工作或是自立门户，努力扬名立万。在战争中很容易掠夺到财富的谣言很快传遍各个角落。很多的年轻人都被当作战士一样去训练。在他们看来，征服其他土地是出人头地的不二选择。

---

rumor *n.* 谣言；传闻   opportunity *n.* 机会

◆ VIKINGS

They invaded other countries with quick attacks from the sea. Their fast boats were called dragons because of the carved dragon's head rising from the bow. The dragon's head warned others of the fierce warriors on board.

Despite all the stories about the warlike Vikings, not all of them were warriors or stayed warriors. After conquering a country or discovering new land, Viking warriors often settled down. They became farmers and traders. These ex-Viking warriors lived much like other people of those times. They became peaceful, *law-abiding* citizens. They worked hard and earned an honest living.

他们以从海上快速进攻的方式入侵其他国家。他们的快船被称为龙舟，因为船头刻的是龙头。这个龙头同时也警告了其他人这艘船上有很勇猛的战士。

尽管所有的故事都讲维京人很好战，但不是所有的维京人都是战士和驻守的战士。在征服一个国家或发现新大陆之后，维京战士经常会居住在那里，然后成为农民和商人。这些曾经的维京战士像那个时期的其他人一样生活着，变成了和平守法的市民。他们努力工作，通过诚实的劳动养家糊口。

---

despite *prep.* 尽管　　　　　　　　　　law-abiding *adj.* 守法的

ADVENTURE TRIP II

♦ VIKINGS

A New Land Is Discovered

One brave Viking, Gardard Svarvarsson, sailed beyond the areas where other Europeans had settled. He was looking for new lands to explore. His travels took him far to the north and west. After days at sea, he found a large island. The weather on the island was cold and *harsh*. Today, the island he discovered is known as Iceland. Not a bad name for a place so cold.

Later, another Viking explorer from Norway, Folke Vilgerdsson, decided to build a *settlement* on Iceland. Some would say he had no choice. He had been booted out of his homeland of Norway by the

---

发现新大陆

有一个勇敢的维京人格达德·赛维安孙，他航行越过了欧洲人居住的区域。他在寻找新的陆地去探索，分别向北和向西航行了很远。经过在海上多天的航行后，他发现了一座大的岛屿，岛上的天气寒冷且严酷。他当时所发现的岛屿正是我们今天所知道的冰岛。用这个名字命名这么冷的地方很贴切。

不久之后，另一个来自挪威的维京人——福克·外尔杰德森——决心要在冰岛上建造住宅。有些人会说他这么做是因为被自己的祖国——挪威

---

harsh *adj.* 严酷的   settlement *n.* （尤指拓荒安家的）定居点

ADVENTURE TRIP II

king. He and his family did not agree with the king's policies. They posed a threat to the king, who was a ruthless, power-hungry ruler.

The king had little *tolerance* for those who did not follow his rules. Rather than risk being *overthrown*, the king ordered Folke, and many of those who agreed with him, out of Norway. Folke, and many of the families sent away from Norway, sailed to Iceland. They set up a settlement on the island. Within 50 years, 400 people had settled on Iceland.

These people of Iceland set up one of the first *democracies*. A democracy is a form of government where people can vote on issues, laws, and rulers. According to democracy, the majority vote

---

的国王撵了出来，所以别无选择，他和他的家人都不赞成国王的政策，他们对这个冷酷且强权的统治者构成了威胁。

国王无法忍受那些不遵从他统治的人。为了巩固政权，他下令让福克和那些与他有同样想法的人离开挪威。福克和许多被赶出挪威的家庭向冰岛航行。他们在岛上盖房，50年间曾有400人居住在冰岛。

冰岛的这些人建立了一种最早的民主制度。民主制度是一种政治形式，人们可以对重大问题、法律和领导人进行投票。民主制度下，少数服

---

tolerance n. 忍受；容忍   overthrow v. 推翻
democracy n. 民主制度

◆ VIKINGS

wins. The people of Iceland were quite happy with the way their lives were run.

Eric The Red

It seems as though Viking exploration was inspired by men getting the boot. And many of those booted out of the country they were living in sailed west. One such Viking was Eric the Red. Eric constantly found himself in trouble while living in Iceland. His *behavior* reached its worst when he killed three men in a fight. The officials of Iceland had enough of Eric and ordered him to leave.

Eric had heard rumors of land even farther west than Iceland.

从多数。在冰岛的人认为进行投票使他们的生命价值得以实现，为此而感到非常高兴。

红发埃里克

似乎是那些被驱赶的人开始了维京人的探索。他们中的很多人被赶出祖国后都向西航行，其中一个这样的维京人名叫红发埃里克。埃里克在冰岛上生活时，不断陷入麻烦当中。一次他在打斗中杀死了三个人，行为恶劣到了极点。冰岛的官员受够了埃里克，下令让他离开。

埃里克听说了在冰岛以西还有陆地的传言。既然他现在要离开这里，

---

behavior *n.* 行为

ADVENTURE TRIP II

Since he had to leave the island, he set sail for this unknown land. He didn't even know if it existed.

After all, it was only a rumor that he had heard. But to his surprise, Eric found the new land after only two days at sea. He reported back that he had found a land with rich green valleys and plenty of *game* to hunt. Because the land was so green, he named it Greenland.

The next year, Eric returned to Greenland with 25 ships filled with settlers looking to start a new life. The ocean voyage was rough, and those making the voyage were not prepared. Only 14 of the ships survived the journey. The survivors settled in two *separate* villages.

索性就朝着那片未知的陆地航行。他甚至不知道是否存在这样一片土地。

毕竟那只是他听到的一个传言，但是令他吃惊的是，在海上航行的两天后他真的发现了新大陆。他回到岛上报告称找到了一片有着绿色山谷和丰富猎物的富饶土地。由于这片土地上植物生长茂盛，所以他给它命名为"格陵兰岛"。

第二年，埃里克带领25艘船的移居者回到格陵兰岛，热切盼望着开始新的生活。然而航海旅途艰苦，埃里克的船队没有做好充分的准备，只有14艘船完成了航行。这些幸存者在岛上建了两个分开的村子，还有教堂

---

game *n.* 猎物　　　　　　　　　　　　　　　separate *adj.* 分开的

They built churches and other buildings. They *set up* a democracy like the one in Iceland. Within ten years, nearly 3,000 brave people had settled in Greenland. They had left everything familiar behind to start a new life in a new land.

Leif Ericson

Perhaps the most famous Viking of all was the second son of Eric the Red. His name was Leif. Because he was Eric's son, he became know as Leif Ericson. Like most Vikings, he was trained to be a warrior and sailor. Because he was the second son, he was given no land to farm when he became older. Rather than hang around

---

和其他一些建筑。他们建立了和冰岛一样的民主制度。10年间，近3 000名勇敢的人居住在格陵兰岛。他们丢下了所熟知的一切，到这个新大陆上开始新的生活。

雷夫·埃里克森

可以说维京人中最出名的是红发埃里克的第二个儿子。他名叫雷夫，因为他是埃里克的儿子，所以被大家称为雷夫·埃里克森。与大多数维京人一样，他被训练成战士和水手。由于他是第二个儿子，所以当他长大以后没有土地可以用来耕种。雷夫不愿在格陵兰岛附近闲逛，他选择了向挪

---

set up　建立

ADVENTURE TRIP II

Greenland, Leif sailed to Norway.

While in Norway, Leif heard about a trader whose ship had been blown way off course in a storm. The story goes on to say that the trader's ship was the first to have spotted the North American coast, even though the trader had no idea of his *location*.

Leif was young and hungry for adventure. He bought the trader's ship and retraced the voyage to this far-away land. Along the way, Leif visited several *coastal* islands. He finally stopped at a place where the land looked welcoming. He called the place Vinland because of all the grapes growing there. To this day, no one knows for sure where Vinland was. It may have been along the eastern edge

威航行。

在挪威的时候，雷夫听说了一个商人的故事。这个商人的船在暴风雨中被吹离了原来的航线。这个故事还说尽管这个商人不知道他所抵达的位置，但这艘商船是第一个发现北美海岸的。

雷夫很年轻并且渴望冒险，他买下了商人的船，沿着他的路线再一次航行到那个遥远的陆地。雷夫沿路游访了许多沿海岛屿。最后他在一个看上去很惹人喜欢的地方停了下来。因为那里长满各种各样的葡萄，所以他称这个地方为"文兰"。直到现在也没有人确切地知道文兰到底在哪。它

location n. 位置   coastal adj. 沿海的

of Canada. Or it may have been in the northeastern United States.

After spending the winter in Vinland, Leif and his crew returned to Greenland. Along the way, Leif discovered a *wrecked* trading vessel and rescued the crew. He was given all the ship's cargo and the nickname Leif the Lucky. When Leif returned to Greenland, he had other things on his mind. He had been *converted* to Christianity by the King of Norway. So he set out to convert the people of Greenland to Christianity.

A love of adventure seemed to be a family trait. While Leif was busy converting Greenlanders to Christianity, his brother, Thorvald,

---

可能在加拿大的东部沿线或者在美国的东北部。

雷夫和船员们在文兰过完冬天后回到了格陵兰岛。沿途，雷夫发现了一艘失事的商船，他救了全体船员的命。被救的人们为了表示感谢，把船上的货物都给了雷夫，并给他起了个昵称"幸运雷夫"。当雷夫返回格陵兰岛时，他又想到了一些其他的事情。由于挪威国王的影响，他已经改信基督教了，所以他打算说服所有格陵兰岛人都改信基督教。

对冒险的钟爱似乎是家族的特点。当雷夫正忙于说服格陵兰岛人改信基督教的时候，他的弟弟索福尔德向他借船。索福尔德想去看看雷夫发现

---

wrecked *adj.* 失事的；遇难的   convert *v.* （使）改变（宗教或信仰）

ADVENTURE TRIP II

asked to borrow Leif's ship. He wanted to see what Leif had discovered. Thorvald and his men sailed along the Vinland coast for two years, exploring the new continent.

One day they came under attack from natives of the area. There was no way these Vikings would back down from a fight, so rather than escape, they stayed to fight. The battle was *tough*, and the natives had the advantage of knowing the land. Leif's brother was killed in this *conflict*, and his body was buried at Vinland. He was the first European known to have died and been buried in North America.

了什么，于是他和他的船员沿着文兰海岸航行了两年，发现了新的大陆。

一天，他们遭到了当地居民的袭击。维京人从不在战争中退却，所以他们没有逃跑，留下来战斗。战争非常艰难，而且当地居民更熟悉地形。雷夫的弟弟在斗争中被杀，尸体就埋在文兰。他是第一个已知的、在战争中牺牲并被葬在北美洲的欧洲人。

---

tough *adj.* 艰难的　　　　　　　　　　　　conflict *n.* 冲突

Other Viking Conquests

The Viking voyages to North America are exciting to us because of how little the Vikings knew about where they were going. Leif and Thorvald Ericson traveled beyond their known world and found a new continent, North America. And it is amazing that it happened 500 years before Columbus was credited with discovering America.

Viking raids into Europe also changed history. They founded states in many different lands. They conquered great nations. And they created an *empire* that lasted well into the 1400s.

维京人的其他征服史

维京人向北美洲航行的事件令我们振奋,因为他们根本不知道自己会走到哪里,就敢于扬帆起航。雷夫和索福尔德·埃里克森在他们未知的领域航行,并发现了新大陆——北美洲。令人称奇的是,这件事发生在哥伦布认为是他发现了美洲的500年以前。

维京人突袭进入欧洲也改变了历史。他们在很多不同的土地上建立政权。他们征服了强大的国家并且建立了一个帝国,这个帝国一直持续到15世纪。

---

empire *n.* 帝国

ADVENTURE TRIP II

For more than 250 years, the Vikings swept into Europe in wave after wave. They were hungry to fight and greedy for riches. They built trade stations along European rivers all the way to the Mediterranean Sea. Viking explorers and raiders even traveled to the Middle East and Asia.

The Vikings were very skilled as sailors. They discovered and settled new lands. Their conquests left lasting marks on our history. *In particular*, they will always be remembered for their bravery and strength in battle, as well as their *fierceness*.

250多年来，维京人一波接着一波地横扫欧洲。他们嗜财贪战，沿着欧洲河岸到地中海沿途都设置了商站。维京探索者和入侵者甚至到达过中东和亚洲。

维京人是非常有经验的水手，他们发现了新陆地并在那儿居住。他们的征服在我们的历史上留下了不可磨灭的印记。特别是他们在战争中的勇敢、毅力，同他们的勇猛一起将一直被人们所牢记。

---

in particular 尤其   fierceness *n.* 勇猛

◆ VIKINGS

Timeline In Viking History

790s..............Viking raids in Europe begin, including Scotland and Ireland

793 ....Viking raid on Lindisfarne *monastery*

844 ....Viking raids on Spain

845 ....Conquest of Hamburg and Paris

856–7, 861 ....Paris conquered by the Vikings

870–930 ....Norse settlement in Iceland

880s..............Harold Finehair attempts to unite Norway

885–6..............Siege of Paris

维京人历史时间表

8世纪90年代……………维京人开始袭击欧洲，包括苏格兰和爱尔兰

793年…………………维京人攻击在林狄斯芬的修道院

844年…………………维京人攻击西班牙

845年…………………攻取德国汉堡和法国巴黎

856年—861年7月…………巴黎被维京人征服

870年—930年 …………挪威人定居冰岛

9世纪80年代……………哈罗德·费恩海尔企图统一挪威

885年—886年 …………围攻巴黎

---

monastery *n.* 修道院

902	Vikings expelled from Dublin
911	*Foundation* of Normandy by Viking chieftain Rollo
912	Viking raiders on the Caspian Sea
917	Refoundation of Viking Dublin
930	Foundation of the Icelandic Althing
980s	Conversion of Russia
985	Eric the Red settles in Greenland
1000	Iceland converted to Christianity; Voyages to Vinland

902年	维京人被驱逐出都柏林
911年	维京首领罗洛建立诺曼底
912年	里海的维京入侵者
917年	重建维京都柏林
930年	冰岛国会成立
10世纪80年代	俄罗斯的转变
985年	红发埃里克定居格陵兰岛
1000年	冰岛人改信基督教；航海到文兰

foundation *n.* 创建

◆ VIKINGS

1066 ....Battle of Stamford Bridge, Battle of Hastings, Norman conquest of England

1066–87 ....William the *Conqueror*, King of England

1091 ....Norman conquest of Sicily

1096–99 ....First crusades

1066年 ······················福桥战役；哈斯汀之役；诺曼征服
1066年—1087年············英国国王征服者威廉
1091年 ······················诺曼征服西西里
1096年—1099年············第一次十字军东征

---

conqueror *n.* 征服者